GROWING WITH GOD

LEARNING TO WALK WITH JESUS

BY BRUCE ROBERTS DREISBACH

To Karl Novak

Your steadfast friendship over thirty years
taught me many of these lessons.

* * *

GROWING WITH GOD

ISBN 978-1467901680

Endorsements for *Growing with God*

"Since beginning his own sojourn of following Jesus out of a totally secular background, Bruce has had a passion to help others do the same. His experience in the "church world" led him to clarify what it means to truly follow Jesus apart from the confusing add-ons of people who are religious but not following Jesus. The disciplines he shares in this book come from what God has to say to us in the Bible and from the heart of one who has patiently and loving mentored many others on the journey. You will find Bruce refreshingly real as a fellow pilgrim as opposed to an arrogant expert telling you what to do. It is a pleasure to travel the path in pursuit of Jesus with him."

>   - *Rev. Patrick Jones, Lead Pastor, Eastern Hills Wesleyan Church, Williamsville, NY*

"God has truly anointed you as a teacher. May the Lord enable this ministry to multiply, because this truth is needed desperately."

>   - *Jack Sullivan, Boston, MA*

"Bruce Dreisbach's teaching is highly effective at equipping believers in the faith. This approach is practical and relevant for today's world. It has inspired our people in their faith and made them much more effective witnesses as well."

>   - *Rev. Richard Rhodes, Pastor of Evangelism, Grace Chapel, Lexington, MA*

Endorsements for Lifestyle Witnessing Seminars

"I've been a Christian all my life and always felt bad I wasn't better at sharing my faith. Understanding that God has made me to witness, rather than evangelize has freed me to share effectively. I've seen more people come to faith in the past three years through *Lifestyle Witnessing* than I have in the previous 70 years of my life. And I've been able to help my friends learn to do the same thing!"

> - *Dick Armstrong, Wheaton Bible Church, Wheaton, IL*

"Your teaching convinced me that my personal mission field is my neighbors and a few special people god has already put in my life. I'm already praying and loving and looking forward to seeing God touch their lives."

> - *Julie Hansen, Phoenix, AZ*

"God has gifted Bruce Dreisbach with the ability to teach, and through *Lifestyle Witnessing* has gifted the church with practical ways for connecting with people and introducing them to Jesus. This course leaves Christians with a renewed desire to witness and with biblical and relevant tools to make the witness effective."

> - *Bishop Richard D. Snyder, Free Methodist Church of North America*

Contents

Introduction

Is faith something like a multiple vitamin? Some people think it is. You take your multiple vitamin daily, even though you are not really sure of what's in it. You take it, even though you are not sure what it's supposed to do nor do you know how it will accomplish that undefined result. You just have a vague hope that if you take it every day, then you will run faster, jump higher, last longer – in short, you'll be healthier, a better person, and enjoy a better life.

When some people first meet Jesus and start to walk down the road of faith, they think it's much like taking a multiple vitamin. "It is not really clear what faith is supposed to do in my life, but I guess I hope if I take a little each day, my life will gradually improve. Somehow I'll become a better person, I'll get a better grip on my understanding of life, and in some vague undefined way, my life will turn out better for having had regular doses of faith."

This is an interesting notion, but it is not at all true. God has a very specific purpose for our walk of faith. It is designed to transform our lives. We become, over the course of time, dramatically new versions of our former selves. We discover a purpose and a giftedness that allows us to change our world and impact the lives of others as we walk with Jesus. In fact, his ultimate goal is for us to become more and more like Jesus. We still have our own unique personality, but our character becomes more like Jesus.

Think for a moment about why God created us. God does not need us. He is self- sufficient. He created the world and everything in it. He sustains the life of the world and intervenes in the history of mankind as he chooses. He enjoys perfect community – with the three persons of the Trinity – the Father, Son, and

Holy Spirit. God does not need us, but He goes to all the trouble to create us and redeem us because he wants to enjoy a relationship with each of us.

Now if these were God's only objectives, to make us more like Jesus and to enjoy a relationship with us, wouldn't it be a lot easier to take us straight to heaven the instant we accepted Jesus? That way God would not have to deal with the problems from our old life, the effects of our repeated sin and failure, nor the stresses and strains of our daily bodily needs. "ZAP!" and we're in heaven! We get new heavenly bodies, we leave all of the past behind and we can learn to be more like Jesus – well, from Jesus himself!

That would be nice, but it is not God's plan for us. God actually has a lot that he wants to accomplish **_in us_** and **_through us_** here in this life before we get to go off to heaven. Yes, God wants to enjoy a growing relationship with us as we learn to walk through life with Jesus. He also wants to bless us. God has many good gifts he gives us here on earth (Jesus called these gifts together the "abundant life"), which are designed to help us become spiritually mature. These gifts are given for our benefit but also so that we may become a blessing to others. God has created each one of us with a special calling and purpose in the world. Part of his goal for our life in him is that we discover our reason for being and participate in some small way in God's great redemptive work in the world.

The objective of this book is to encourage you to learn six disciplines that will help you develop a healthy spiritual life. By learning these disciplines and making them part of your life you will discover the "abundant life" Jesus has promised to give everyone who trusts him and follows him. Adopting these spiritual habits will allow you to live life in Jesus to the full and to reach all of your God-given potential.

Several years ago I read a story about a woman who passed away in the Flatbush section of Brooklyn, New York. Ellen Esterbrook was a poor, single woman in her late sixties when she died. She lived in a small walk up studio apartment in a fairly rundown section of Flatbush. Her neighbors described her as a very frugal woman, saving twist ties, washing out and reusing her bread bags. She collected aluminum cans in her small wire shopping cart and dragged them up the five flights of steps to her apartment every day. She sold these to supplement her Social Security check. According to the coroner's office, when she died she was underweight and close to being malnourished. To some degree her death was precipitated by her poor physical condition.

When authorities went through her personal effects, they were amazed to discover that Ms. Esterbrook had left an estate of about $1.8 million. She had no heirs and no will so eventually this large sum will be divided up between various government agencies. Further research uncovered the fact that Ellen had been raised in a good family and had finished college. When her father died, he left her about $200,000, which she invested in the stock market. Through very shrewd investments over the years, she had been able to parlay her initial capital into $1.8 million. For most of her life, this woman lived in a chronic state of near poverty even though she was actually quite rich.

The sad fact is that many believers live in a state of chronic spiritual poverty, even though they have been given "abundant life" – spiritual riches beyond our wildest dreams. Much like Ms. Esterbrook, even though they are spiritually wealthy, they live in self imposed poverty, never learning how to tap into the spiritual wealth God's given them. Some fail to access their spiritual wealth out of ignorance. Others simply neglect to take the time to unlock and use the "abundant life." Finally, some are actually spiritual paupers by choice – even after learning of the spiritual riches God has bestowed on them, they continue to live in their old lifestyle of poverty. Perhaps these people are more comfortable with the poverty they have always known and prefer it to the unknown of being spiritually rich.

My hope and prayer are that as you read this small volume you will learn of the spiritual riches God has given you in Jesus Christ. My goal is to teach you how to develop the six disciplines that will release the "abundant life" into your life experience. My prayer is that your life will overflow with the richness of Christ that you will find your purpose in the world, and your life will have a profound impact on those around you.

Chapter 1 – Life is a Risk

There are times when I feel like an accidental tourist in my own life. I certainly did not expect to be in the place I find myself, nor did I ever imagine this is what my life would look like at this point in time. Life is full of unforeseen developments. The older I get, the more I find this to be true. Why does this observation come as such a surprise? It's really the American Dream that's messing with our heads. We've been raised on this naive and untrue notion that the world is full of good things and all you have to do is reach out and you can grab your share of "the good life." We have these expectations that life should be full of new cars, nice houses, people who love and admire us, jobs which are fulfilling, perfect health and plenty of leisure time to enjoy the blessings of the American Dream.

The truth is – life is fragile and quite unpredictable. Yes, there is much that is good and sweet, but there are a multitude of things that can happen that just knock our legs out from under us. The world is a dangerous place. Things happen as you live life. As Bilbo Baggins said, "It's a risky business going out your front door." Life can be pleasant, but it can also be full of trauma and hurt. Some of the things that put stress in our lives are of our own making. Often we make mistakes, bad decisions, personal choices that have very negative consequences. Other hard and painful things are forced on us by circumstances beyond our control. We are innocent victims, but the anguish is just as real. We are all just trying to find our way in a lost and hurting world. Some of us start life with a lot of positive advantages. Others are saddled with some serious obstacles to overcome. No matter how we begin life or where we stand today, we are all at-risk.

As believers in Jesus Christ we have been given a rich treasure trove of spiritual resources. These spiritual benefits give us the potential to rise above the challenges of life and to help us find the sweet and the good in ourselves and in the world around us. But simply knowing Jesus is not enough. We need to learn about these spiritual resources and make them a part of our lives to reap the blessings God intends for us. A believer who remains passive or simply ignores the principles for living life to the full can miss out on all the abundance God intends to give us in life. Not only can we miss the good, we can still choose the bad. This freedom to choose gives us the opportunity to experience more joy and fulfillment than we can possibly imagine in life. This freedom also holds the potential for choices that lead to unmitigated disaster and despair.

A TALE OF TWO WOMEN

Agnes Bojaxhiu was born in 1910 in the little town of Skopje, which was then in Yugoslavia. As a child, Agnes was drawn to God. Her relationship grew through out her adolescence and at 18 she decided to become a nun, joining the sisters of Loreto in 1928. After a number of years of training, Agnes became a teaching sister and was assigned to several schools. In 1946 she was sent as a missionary to teach in a convent school in Calcutta, India. The growth of her spiritual disciplines gave her a heart that was tender towards both God and the needs of people around her. One day she came across a half- dead woman lying in front of a Calcutta hospital. She was moved with compassion and stayed with the woman until she died.

This experience began a transformation of her life. Her increasing contact with the dying poor on the streets of India led her to the conviction that "the worst poverty wasn't material but the total abandonment by others." [1] She had found her calling. In 1950, Mother Theresa founded an order of missionary nuns called the Missionaries of Charity. Over the past 50 years this order has grown from 12 sisters to over 3,000 now serving in 517 missions throughout 100 countries worldwide. Together the sisters of this Order feed over 500,000 families and help 90,000 lepers each year.

Marion Landis was born in the rolling farm country of eastern Pennsylvania in 1926. She and her parents attended a modest sized mainline church in her small town while growing up. Many of the better people in town attended this church, but Marion always felt like a social inferior. After all, her Dad was only a barber and her Mom was a secretary at the pretzel factory. In adulthood Marion and her husband joined the local Quaker meeting. Marion had strong religious feelings but no particular religious convictions. She became involved in the fight for civil rights, fair housing practices, and other worthy social justice causes. These interests allowed her to fit well within the Society of Friends.

At the age of 43, Marion met Jesus and committed her life to following him. As a new believer she sought out fellowship, joined a woman's Bible study, and transferred to a church that featured good teaching in the Scriptures. For ten years she was involved in a number of activities which encouraged her spiritual growth and allowed her to reach out and care for others. Then something began to change. She spent more time reading paperback romance novels and less time in the Scriptures. She spent less time in fellowship with other believers and more time watching afternoon soap operas on TV. Her priorities began to shift from the Lord and the needs of others to herself.

One summer she had an emotional affair with an older man she met at the YMCA. This began to undermine her relationship with her husband. Her soaps and pulp novels convinced her she "deserved more from life." At the age of 59, after 36 years of marriage, she moved out and announced she wanted a divorce. Three weeks later she decided that might have been a terrible mistake, but the damage was done. After her divorce, she lived alone in a constantly shrinking circle of family and friends. Her self-pity and self-absorption eventually destroyed her family and almost every relationship she had built during her lifetime. When she died at age 79 she was truly alone and unloved. Not abandoned, like the women Mother Theresa cared for, but isolated by the bad choices she had made during the last 20 years of her life.

Life is risky. God loves us so much he has given us the freedom to choose. We have the freedom to choose a relationship with God through Jesus Christ. When we trust Jesus, we are given the Holy Spirit to guide us and lead us. We are also given enormous spiritual resources, which Jesus called "abundant life." But to reap the benefits of these blessings, we have to learn some spiritual disciplines. We need to practice these habits and keep them a healthy part of our lives. Spiritual disciplines – that's the reason for the difference in the outcome of Mother Theresa's life and that of Marion Landis. One set of choices leads to a life lived with power, with joy, with an impact on others that will last into eternity. The other set of choices leads to the destruction of all we hold dear, our entire life wasted and thrown away. Our salvation is secure but the life God gave us on this earth is a complete loss.

BUILD YOUR LIFE ON THE ROCK

Faith is a journey, not a destination. God has given each of us a distinctive set of circumstances to cope with in life. He has also given each of us unique gifts and skills to help us deal with our life situation. The spiritual resources Jesus gives each follower allow us to overcome obstacles, meet challenges and cope with adversity as we travel through the journey of life. Jesus said how well we use our spiritual resources to leverage our skills and circumstances on the road of life, is like building a house. He told his followers, "Everyone who hears these words of mine and puts them into practice is like a wise man who built his house on the rock. The rain came down, the streams rose, and the winds blew and beat against that house; yet it did not fall, because it had its foundation on the rock. But everyone who hears these words of mine and does not put them into practice is like a foolish man who built his house on sand. The rain came down, the streams rose, and the winds blew and beat against that house, and it fell with a great crash." Matt 7:24-27

Life is a risky business. The world is not a safe place. I know it. You know it. God knows it. But the good news I want to share with you through this book is that God is fully committed to helping you and me through all the risky, dangerous, tough spots in life. In Jesus we have the opportunity to access God's love and power to meet the demands of everyday life in a way that is simply not possible on our own.

Jesus is God's way to reestablish a personal relationship between each of us and God, our Heavenly Father. As we learn to walk with Jesus each day, through both the good times and the hard times that will come, we can discover a rich resource of spiritual power and strength that will transform us into the people we want to be, the people God created us to be. Jesus tells his followers, "I have come in order that you may have life—life in all its fullness." (John 10:10) This abundant life is available as a free gift to everyone who trusts Jesus and follows him into a relationship with God. It does not guarantee a life of riches, or success, or the elimination of problems, difficulty, and pain. But it does assure of us of God's commitment to unleash his awesome love, grace, and power into our lives in such a way that all of our life is radically transformed. Into a life that is deeper, richer and more fulfilling than we could ever hope or wish for.

JESUS - THE GREAT EQUILIZER

We all begin the journey of life with a variety of advantages and obstacles. Our birth family, our parenting, our social-economic status, our ethnic heritage, and our geographic location – all these factors play a major part in how we begin in life. Our physical appearance: Heights, weight, hair color, looks, health, intelligence – these and other factors have a marked impact on our start on the journey of life. These are not factors we have any control over. You and I never asked to be born into these particular circumstances. Some of us were born into situations of great love and blessing. Others of us were born into difficult or even tragic circumstances. You may begin life as an innocent victim.

The good news is that no matter how you got started, or even the difficult circumstances you find yourself now, God can take these circumstances and through the power of the Holy Spirit, he can transform them into blessing. Jesus is the great equalizer. No matter how good or how bad our original circumstances, when we begin to walk with him, he transforms each of us into dramatically better people. His promise to each of us who trust him: "And we know that in all things God works for the good of those who love him, who have been called according to his purpose….What, then, shall we say in response to this? If God is for us, who can be against us? He who did not spare his own Son, but gave him up for us all-how will he not also, along with him, graciously give us all things?" (Romans: 28:31,32)

I, like many of you, am an innocent victim. I was born into a highly dysfunctional family system, one that may have been the result of generations of abuse. My home was a fearful place to be a child. When I was seven years old, I remember my father getting angry over some petty infraction of the rules he lived by. He coldly and calmly made me take off all my clothes except for my underpants. "Everything you have is mine, and I have given it to you!" He said, "You own nothing and deserve nothing! But I'm going to be kind, and let you keep your underpants! Now you are on your own!" With that he tossed me out of the house and locked all the doors. I spent several hours in my front yard in full view of the neighbors, crying and screaming my heart out, wearing only my underpants, begging and pleading to be let back in. You might say that my father practiced a rather severe form of conditional love, if you can call it love at all, in our home.

Growing with God

By the time I reached adolescence, pain and anger formed such a penetrating fog in my soul. I could hardly get through a day without lashing out at someone or something to try to deal with my emotional turmoil. Jesus transformed those feelings and gave me a peace and a calm from the first days I walked with him. Over time, he's addressed and healed many of those deep emotional wounds I had when I first came to him. Looking back, I marvel at the deep healing God has brought to my life through my faith walk with Jesus. I was very lonely. My childhood insecurity had created an inability to build and maintain healthy relationships. Not only was I lost and lonely before I met Jesus, I felt a tremendous desire to belong and be accepted by some group of people. In Christ I have discovered the power of friendship with Jesus himself to help my loneliness. He has also created a wide network of friends and family for me that has matured and sustained my spiritual growth as an adult. I now have a safe place of belonging.

In Jesus I've discovered purpose and meaning in my life. I no longer feel like I am drifting alone and helpless down a river of circumstances and events I am powerless to control. I know who I am, where I have come from, what God created me to do, the gifts and talents he's given me to work with, and the eternal destiny and purpose of my life. My work and my life have purpose, and they bring me joy in the journey.

Jesus has transformed my love life. From a raging teenage sexaholic with every prospect of becoming a lifelong cad and womanizer, Jesus has remade me from the inside out. He has turned me into a loving, faithful, encouraging husband of one woman for over 35 years. He's blessed me with a marriage relationship and best friend in my wife which is better than I could have ever dreamed of.

My childhood was a black pit with depths of despair I have never been able to fully understand, nor am I sure I want to. But in spite of that handicap, Jesus has transformed me into a father who has been able to provide a loving, grace filled, carefree, and safe childhood for both of my daughters. Now adults, they each have a strong love relationship with Jesus and are wonderful, mature women in their own right. To this day, we have a precious love between us because God was able to transform me into their Daddy.

Finally, as I have confronted major and minor challenges, relational problems, career choices, and decisions of many kinds, I have always found Jesus true to his word. He is available 24 hours a day, seven days a week, to provide guidance, wisdom, and direction, in any way that I need. His willingness to help me out in the small details of daily life, as well as the major turning points, has been a source of constant assurance and encouraged the growth of a rich and healthy spiritual life over decades.

When I look back over my life walking with Jesus, I can say with Martin Luther King, "I ain't what I want to be, I ain't what I'm gonna be, but thank God I ain't what I used to be." This is God's promise to every believer, "If anyone is in Christ, he is a new creation; the old has gone, the new has come! (2 Cor 5:17) God promises that no matter how good or bad our circumstances, he can transform them and make us into better people. He promises to pour out his blessing and fill our lives with a richness of joy and hope. This book will help you learn the spiritual disciplines that will allow this gift of "abundant life" to take root, grow, and overflow in your life.

Discussion Questions – Chapter 1

1) Describe the "warmest" room in your house during your childhood years. Feel free to interpret "warmest" as you like.

2) Has life, so far, turned out like you expected? Explain your answer.

3) Was there a time in your life when you first became aware that there may be meaning in life that is larger than yourself? Describe your "Ah ha!" moment.

4) Describe a relationship that helped you grow in your faith journey. What did that person do for you that was helpful to your growth & maturity?

5) Was there a part of the reading in this chapter that was particularly helpful for you, that made a connection in your mind, or that you disagree with? Share about that.

6) How might you use what you learned in this chapter to change your life in the coming week or months?

Growing with God

Chapter 2 – Starting Your Spiritual Journey

ASKING THE RIGHT QUESTIONS

There are times in everyone's life, when we stop in front of the mirror and do a double take at the person staring back at us. We pause and some inner voice causes us to ask ourselves some rather penetrating questions. "Who am I? Why am I here? Where is my life going? What does my life mean? Why do I exist? Whom do I belong with? Who do I want to belong to? What does my future hold?"

At various times in our lives, each of us experiences periods of searching. What is it we are searching for? Many Americans are searching for meaning or purpose in their lives. Others are seeking to be loved. More than anything, they want to be known, named, recognized, accepted, and enfolded. Others are looking for the satisfaction of achieving something noteworthy or simply worthwhile. They want their lives to make a difference in the world. Some are searching for healing and solace from deep wounds that have been inflicted upon them by others. They desire security, belonging, peace, and safety in a troubled world.

I believe that while the motivation driving our search varies, each of us at times, are involved in this search for something more. Blaise Paschal captures the nature of our human search for something more in his notion that within every human heart there lies an infinite God-shaped void only God can fill. Our search is the result of our trying to use many temporal, lesser things, to fill this inner need only God can satisfy. Paschal says, "These things are all inadequate because the infinite abyss [in our souls] can only be filled by an infinite [relationship], that is to say only by God himself."[2]

We launch fresh from childhood into the adult world with a passionate desire to find that which will center our being and help us achieve a sense of balance and well-being. Rarely is this easy. One speaker described his generation (Generation X) this way: "One third of my generation was aborted before being born. Of those who lived, half were raised in a broken home. One third of the survivors have been abused—physically, sexually, or emotionally." These are tough conditions to use as a launching pad for life.

It is easy to see that the majority of Americans under the age of 40 have been through traumatic experiences. If they were perfectly honest, most Americans today would admit they grew up in a dysfunctional family. In our day and age, dysfunction is a normative background experience. The causes of family dysfunction can vary widely. It could be divorce, physical or sexual abuse, substance abuse, workaholicism, materialism, emotional abuse, or neglect, but regardless of the root causes, the basic rules of the dysfunctional family are the same: "Don't talk; don't trust; don't feel."

If you grew up in a dysfunctional home, you absorbed these basic ground rules for life and relationships. Frankly, these operating rules, even if they are quite unconscious, do a real disservice to our search for that which will provide fulfillment and satisfaction for our lives. Many of us spend years wondering, questioning, and struggling to figure out how to connect the dots in life.

SEARCHING FOR HOME

Our search in life is a spiritual search. To find wholeness and health as an adult, we must own our inner divine spark that allows us to rise to our full potential as human beings. It is this search I call *seeking home*. This spiritual home we are seeking is a matter of the heart. Home is in our hearts. Home is the conviction, the awareness, that we are beings with a higher purpose. It is the place we are all looking for where we can be accepted. When we are where we feel we belong. It is a place of unconditional love. We experience relationships that fill our life with positive meaning. There is a sense of inner peace and prosperity regardless of the storms of life raging in our current circumstances or in the world around us.

No matter how difficult, painful, or damaged your childhood, as an adult you have the chance to find a new home--a spiritual home that will transform both your current experience of life and all of your future for the better. I'm convinced almost every person has an inner voice telling him or her that "today is the first day of the rest of my life." No matter how dark and difficult your past and present, God offers new hope each day. He spurs us into a spiritual search to find a better place—a place we can really call home and find the person we were meant to be.

However, in this search for meaning, purpose, love, relationship, and belonging, we often get confused and misdirected. As the old cowboy lament points out, we are looking for love, but in all the wrong places. In the same way we are looking for spiritual wholeness and health. But rather than seeking a relationship with God himself, we end up trying to find meaning and satisfaction in lesser alternatives offered by our world. It may be worthwhile to stop and ask yourself: "What am I counting on to find personal satisfaction or fulfillment from?" These could be good things—helping others in need, building a tight group of friends, a rewarding career, a loving relationship, seeking to be maximized as an individual or contributing in some significant way to a good cause. Or you could be seeking escape and solace in some bad habits: alcohol or drug use, sex and pornography, isolation, or unhealthy relationships.

TRUSTING JESUS

These issues and a variety of other temporary sources of satisfaction or solace are simply detours in the quest for spiritual wholeness and health. In my book, *Exploring God without Getting Religious*, I talk in more detail about some of these detours and then delve into how we can have a relationship with God through Jesus Christ. For a more detailed explanation of this topic, please refer to that volume, especially Chapters 10 – 13. For now, I'll give a quick overview in hopes that it will be helpful to some readers.

The facts of the Incarnation are fairly simple to understand. They are, however, radical and life changing in their implications. God is in the business of intervening in our world and in changing lives, even today. The way he has chosen to do it is through Jesus. In Jesus we find the God who is willing to come to us, to hang out with us, to be our friend, and our savior on terms that we can understand. Jesus was a real historical figure. He is alive today and with the Holy Spirit, he demonstrates God's commitment to be available to us 24 hours a day, seven days a week. He is truly God with us.

God's gift of a new life, a new relationship through Jesus is free. No strings attached. "It is by God's grace that you've been saved by faith. It is not the result of your own efforts, but God's gift so that no one can boast about it." (Ephesians 2:8) Jesus tells us that if we believe in him and trust our lives into his hands, he will give us abundant life today and eternal life forever. He promises a new birth, a spiritual birth—and it depends entirely on him and not at all on me. There is nothing I can do to add to God's grace and to facilitate the process.

Jesus has made a way where there was no way. That is the good news, the Gospel. Jesus has created a spiritual bridge we can walk over into a life of forgiveness, healing, and restoration as we experience a personal relationship with a gracious, loving, heavenly Father. It is a free gift! But like any gift, we have to decide to reach out and accept it.

It is simple to do, walking over this bridge. Even a child can do it—it is that easy. It doesn't depend at all on our ability, our maturity, or our worthiness. We don't need to know or understand Scripture. We don't need to attend church. It is a free gift.

You can accept this free gift right now wherever you are. Simply stop and talk to your heavenly Father: "Dear God, I admit I have sinned and fallen short and that I am separated from you. I want to accept the free gift of life in Jesus. I put my life in your hands and trust you as my Savior. Thank you for loving me and for giving me the gift of new life--both now and forever. I pray this in Jesus' name. Amen."

BEGINNING STEPS

Let's talk about what happens after you accept the free gift of Jesus' love. In reality, there is no one "normative experience." There is almost as much variation in one's initial response to beginning the walk of faith, as there are people who populate the world today. God has made each of us unique. I don't know why, with six billion people in the world. If it had been left up to me, I probably would have offered seven different models and three color choices, much like a suburban developer. Not God. He makes every snowflake unique. He makes each one of us unique. It should not come as a surprise that there is no standard experience you should expect after trusting Jesus. Some find a tremendous sense of relief as the burden of guilt, pain, and fear is lifted off their shoulders. Others have a quiet, glowing peace that begins to fill and to penetrate all aspects of their lives. Some have a powerful emotional experience—almost a "rush" or a high of spiritual power and cleansing released in their lives. Many others, me included, experience no emotion at all.

Reggie Morgan, who we met in *Exploring God without Getting Religious*, demonstrates the power of Jesus to have an immediate impact on a life. Raised in the home of an angry alcoholic father and a codependent mother, Reggie's life was a fortress built to keep people out of his life and to keep himself safe—from other people. When Reggie gave his life to Jesus and started to walk with him, he experienced dramatic changes from the start. He shares, "When I trusted Jesus, I was overwhelmed with two feelings. I was engulfed with a profound sense of peace, and I realized I was no longer alone. It was the first time in my adult life that I felt safe, loved, and accepted."

Reggie's friend Lyn, who met Jesus a couple of years later, describes her experience. "I felt like I had been given a fresh start. I have always been a terrible worry-wart at times, but now it was different. I know now that the wonderful peacefulness I felt was the grace of God."

My own beginning was not emotional at all. I just found myself curious about how this whole "God thing" was supposed to work. If you asked me to explain the difference between walking through life, talking to myself and praying to God, I would have had difficulty explaining it. Yet I had this incredible sense God was actually answering my prayers! Over that first year as a believer, I felt I got the wisdom I needed, and God opened doors before me until it became clear that not only could he hear my prayers, he seemed to be using them to bless my life.

Whatever your particular experience, there are some beginning steps that will prove helpful in your spiritual growth. To begin with, you are going to have a ton of questions. That's great. You have a lot to learn. You need to keep in mind though, that it takes a lifetime to grow a life. Do not get overwhelmed by the fact that you have more questions than answers. You don't have the *Dummy's Guide to All of Life's Problems*. You have a **relationship** with Jesus. You are like a little child. Work on taking baby steps as you begin to explore your new world of faith. Keep asking your questions, both to God in prayer and to your friends who know

Jesus. Your doubts and questions don't threaten God; they are simply a means he can use to help you grow in your faith.

One of the best sources of information is the Bible. Get a New Testament in a modern translation, which will be easier to understand. Good translations to start with might be *The Good News Version*, the *New International Version* (NIV), or *The Message* (a paraphrase). We will talk more about how to learn from the Bible further on, but for starters read the Gospels (Matthew, Mark, Luke and John), which contain the life and teachings of Jesus.

There are also some books that can give you a more detailed discussion of faith and how to grow in your relationship with God. Three good volumes I recommend for beginners include: *Mere Christianity* by C.S. Lewis; *The Case for Christ* by Lee Strobel; and *Christianity for Skeptics* by Steve Kumar.

FORGIVENESS

As a new believer, one of the things that will surprise you the most is your continuing tendency to mess up. Maybe not. I suppose it depends on your view of how well you are doing. If you are a perfectionist, any minor flaw or failure will strike you as a capital offense. "Gee, if I'm a new person in Christ (see 2 Cor.5:17) how can this be happening to me?" On the other hand, if you have low self-esteem, you may be struck by the good things that happen once you start to walk with Jesus. Here is the truth. I'm a mess, you're a mess, but it's ok. We all fall short, but God's grace has us covered.

Once you trust Jesus, his death on the cross covers all the sin, failure, and mistakes in your life. This includes those past, those you make today, and those you make in the future. Jesus pays the bill and it's done. "But if we walk in the light, as he is in the light, we have fellowship with one another, and the blood of Jesus, his Son, purifies us from all sin. (1 John 1:7) Does that mean we become perfect? Sorry, it does not. The hard truth is that as long as we are upon this earth, we will be wrestling with our sinful nature.

As followers of Jesus, we don't become perfect people. We are still people prone to failure, like everybody else, but we are saved. That means our sins are forgiven, our relationship with God has been restored, and we have the Holy Spirit living in us. His job is to teach us, guide us and help us to grow. God's goal is that we become more like Jesus every year we are on earth. But perfection – that will have to wait for heaven. The Apostle John pinpoints our condition when he says, "If we claim to be without sin, we deceive ourselves and the truth is not in us." (1 John 1:8)

When I started to follow Jesus, I was coming out of a life of sex, drugs, and rock n roll. I was a chronic liar, stealing was an ingrained habit, and I was a womanizer. Honestly, as I look back at my early walk with Jesus, sitting around naked at Woodstock, smoking pot, and enjoying the music with my hippie friends, I was not very sensitive to the sin in my life. As I grew with God, he began to weed out the most obvious problem areas. As I've walked with Jesus over the years, looking back I see he has taken care of a lot of the more obvious sins in my life. At the same time I've become much more sensitive to sin so there are still issues (perhaps less visible to the public eye) that the Holy Spirit keeps working on in my walk with God.

So what do you do when you mess up? God's word is quite clear on this point. The Apostle John wrote these words to guide us, "My dear children, I write this to you so that you will not sin. But if anybody does sin, we have one who speaks to the Father in our defense - Jesus Christ, the Righteous One. He is the atoning sacrifice for our sins, and not only for ours but also for the sins of the whole world."(1 John 2:1, 2) We simply need to talk to God about it. First we repent, which is just another way of saying that we acknowledge the error and want to make it right. Then we ask God for forgiveness. John goes on to say, "If we confess our sins, he is faithful and just and will forgive us our sins and purify us from all unrighteousness. (1 John 1:9) Finally we accept that he has forgiven us. Scripture says when God forgives our sins he buries them deeper than the bottom of the sea, or as far as the east is from the west. They are forgiven, forgotten and gone forever.

God is fully committed to the success of our new relationship with him. He will not let our sin and failures get in the way of the process of healing, transformation, and maturing he has designed for us. Through our walk with Jesus, God is able to constantly encourage us, guide us and correct us to keep us on the road that leads to wholeness and spiritual health. God not only has a wonderful end result in mind. He has so designed the process that each step in our journey opens door after door of blessing and satisfaction that we can experience every day of our life on earth as well as through all eternity. Jesus is the key to discovering God's good gift of "abundant life."

<u>Discussion Questions – Chapter 2</u>

1) What is your favorite season of the year and why?

2) Have you ever been given a gift that you felt had "strings attached?" How did that make you feel?

3) What is the best gift anyone has ever given you? Why was that one so special?

4) We all struggle with trying to find meaning and purpose in life in the wrong places. If you are willing, share about one of these times in you own life where you sought blessing from something or someone other than God.

5) How confident do you feel in your relationship with Jesus? Do you know that your house is built upon the rock? If not, just pray the prayer found at the bottom of page 10. Do it right now!

6) Where do you see yourself in your relationship with Jesus today? Briefly try to characterize your current walk with him.

7) How could you use what you learned in this chapter to change your life in the coming week?

Chapter 3 – The Abundant Life

LIVING WITH JESUS

What's it like to have an ongoing relationship with Jesus? As I mentioned in the beginning of this book, faith is a journey, not a destination. So your relationship with Jesus will grow and develop over time. It may take awhile for you to discern how Jesus is making a difference in your life. Jesus does give his followers some pretty strong indications about what it will be like living with the Lord in your life.

First of all you should anticipate change. "Therefore, if anyone is in Christ, he is a new creation; the old has gone, the new has come!" (2 Cor 5:17) You should anticipate positive change. Jesus said, "Come to me, all you who are weary and burdened, and I will give you rest. Take my yoke upon you and learn from me, for I am gentle and humble in heart, and you will find rest for your souls. For my yoke is easy and my burden is light." (Matt 11:28-30) Finally, you should expect a growing richness to begin to permeate all areas of your life. God wants to have a powerful, transforming impact on every area of our lives. Jesus describes his intentions for his followers in these words: "I have come that they may have abundant life, more and better life than they ever dreamed of." (John 10:10)

The abundant life, which Jesus promises to those who seek him and trust him, is a phrase that describes a vast array of spiritual resources that become ours when we give ourselves to God. What is this abundant life? I cannot describe it in its entirety, because it is a gift God wants to give you in a rather unique way. Jesus calls it "life to the fullest." God will customize this "life" to fit your unique person—so it is not exactly the same for everybody, but there are some common elements, which are described in Scripture. As a follower of Jesus, these are all things God wants to pour into your life, if you will let him.

In giving us "life to the full" God essentially offers to give us what we need to reach our full potential. No matter where we are in life, no matter how many mistakes we've made or bad breaks we've encountered, God is committed to helping us become the person he created us to be. The story of Leslie Smith's life is a great example. She was born and raised in a good family in Pittsburgh, Pennsylvania. One Christmas, she received a chemistry set as a gift. Leslie discovered she had a love and passion for science that motivated her all through high school. She could hardly wait to get to college so she could study to become a real scientist.

College life turned out to be a dramatic turning point in her life – but not for the better. Midway through her freshman year at West Virginia University, Leslie became depressed, attempted suicide and finally dropped out of college. Eventually, she was committed to the psychiatric unit of the Woodville State Hospital in Carnegie, Pennsylvania. The doctors decided she had depression and borderline personality disorder, a pervasive pattern of instability, which includes extreme mood swings, an inability to form lasting relationships and low self-esteem. For the next ten years, Smith drifted between mental institutions and periods of living on the streets as a homeless vagabond.

The low point of her descent into a living hell came in the aftermath of burns suffered when she lit her clothes on fire one night. Rather than ending her life, she suffered excruciating pain for several years from self inflicted wounds over one third of her body. When she was finally released from the burn unit at the Dorothea Dix Psychiatric Hospital, she was befriended by Sister Helen Wright. Sister Helen worked for Urban Ministries, a homeless ministry in Raleigh, North Carolina. Under her loving care, Leslie began to recover from both her external wounds and the deep wounds of her heart. Trusting Jesus and learning to walk with him opened new doors of opportunity for Leslie.

Her path of healing and restoration began when she volunteered to answer telephones for Urban Ministries. Later God opened a door for a job in a lab doing scientific research. The lab encouraged Leslie to take some college science courses. She eventually got a scholarship and earned a degree in biochemistry from Duke. From there she went on to complete medical school at East Carolina University and plans to serve as a doctor with the poor somewhere in Appalachia. She says, "I want to make a difference. I want to show people there is no such thing as hopelessness." Leslie Smith's life is a dramatic testimony to the power of Jesus' abundant life to transform even the most difficult circumstances into God's best. [3]

In Jesus, our relationship with God is characterized by the presence of perfect love and the absence of fear. God's word describes our relationship by saying, "[God's] perfect love casts out fear." (1John 4:18) Jesus says our relationship with God is to be warm and intimate. When we pray to God, he wants us to call him "Daddy" (Luke 11:2, Romans 8:15). And God promises to hear our prayers when we call out to him. "Ask and it will be given to you; seek and you will find; knock and the door will be opened to you. For everyone who asks", Jesus tells his followers, "receives. He who seeks finds; and to him who knocks, the door will be opened." (Matthew 7:7-8)

God knows where we are at and what our lives are like. He is not distant, remote or uninvolved. He is very near, tender, and compassionate. He knows our past, our present, and our future. Jesus says, "Come to me all you who are weary and burdened and I will give you rest. Take my yoke upon you and learn from me, for I am gentle and humble in heart and you will find rest for your souls. For my yoke is easy and my burden light." (Matthew 11:28-30)

We don't need to worry about food, clothing, or paying the rent. God promises to provide for us. Jesus said, "Do not worry about your life, what you will eat or drink; or about your body, what you will wear. Is not life more important than food, and the body more important than clothes? Look at the birds of the air; they do not sow or reap or store away in barns, and yet your heavenly Father feeds them. Are you not much more valuable than they?" (Matt 6:25-27)

THE FOREVER FAMILY

But abundant life involves a lot more than having a love relationship with God, receiving rest and provision for all our needs as well as 24-hour access of supernatural power. God knows that we are feeble and frail, prone to wander, and we often mess up. He provides for that as well. If we make a mistake, hurt someone, fall into sin, he provides a way to make it right. "If we claim to be without sin, we deceive ourselves and the truth is not in us. If we confess our sins, he is faithful and just and will forgive us our sins and purify us from all unrighteousness." (1John 1:8-9)

The abundant life offers benefits that go way beyond you and me as individuals. For one thing, when we trust Jesus we are immediately adopted into God's own family, which is comprised of all of those who know and love him. Granted, the family is made up of people like you and me - homeless orphans Jesus picked up off the street, cleaned up and brought home to be adopted as children into God's family. Our relationship with Jesus not only means we have become heirs with access to vast spiritual riches. We also now have an enormous family—spiritual brothers and sisters, mothers and fathers, aunts and uncles, all over the world who know Christ and who love those whom he has accepted.

If you are like me and grew up without a family or in a family that was relationally broken, this is pretty hard to imagine. But everything you ever wanted a family to be, God's family is for those who trust Jesus. You are no longer alone! You may not know anyone in your new spiritual family yet, but they are all around you. As you begin to grow with God and ask him to connect you to others who love him, you will discover that having brothers and sisters in Christ is one of the richest blessings of the abundant life.

In addition to complete access to God and a family we can turn to, Jesus gives us the Holy Spirit to teach us and guide us every day. The Holy Spirit is the third person of God. Jesus says he won't leave us as orphans when he goes to sit at the right hand of the Father, but he will send us the Holy Spirit to live with us and in us. "The Holy Spirit will teach you all things and remind you of everything I have said to you." (John 14:15-21, 25-27) "He will guide you into all truth." (John 15:26-27, John 16:5-15)

So God wants to give us his wisdom every day in every situation we encounter in life. He gives us his love, his peace and his joy all in a form we can take with us at all times. The Apostle Paul called this "Christ in me," and it gives all believers spiritual resources for today and hope of glory that is to come in eternal life. The abundant life provides amazing resources. If you learn the six spiritual disciplines we are about to explore, you can have the abundant life welling up to overflowing. Jesus says these spiritual benefits will be like water to a thirsty man. "Jesus stood and said in a loud voice, "If anyone is thirsty, let him come to me and drink. Whoever believes in me, as the Scripture has said, streams of living water will flow from within him." By this he meant the Spirit, whom those who believed in him were later to receive."(John 7:37-39)

MAKING A DIFFERENCE FOR ETERNITY

What is the result of living the abundant life? It is to have a profound and positive impact on the lives of people in your world. The point of abundant life is not just to bless each of us with untold riches for living everyday—although it does do that. Jesus said if we remain in him and drink of the abundant life he offers us, we would have lives of fruitfulness. We will have a profound impact on the lives of others around us.

This spiritual impact is seen in changed lives. If you want to invest wisely, invest in that which will bear fruit both today and in eternity. What's that? It is investing in God's love and in the people he loves. All those he's created on earth, whether they know him yet or not, are the object of his attention and concern. When we make ourselves available, we will see much spiritual fruit in the lives of people. Jesus said, "Remain in me, and I will remain in you. No branch can bear fruit by itself; it must remain in the vine. Neither can you bear fruit unless you remain in me." (John 15:1-17)

One way to view the story of Leslie Smith is through her eyes – the perspective of the person who was lost and broken who has been found by Jesus. The Lord healed Leslie, redeemed her life, gave her a fresh start, and helped her back onto the road of becoming the person God created her to be. The other lens to view this story is through the eyes of Sister Helen Wright. Helen was given the opportunity to reach out and love a lost, broken child that God was desirous of saving. Helen's love helped Leslie move though a period of healing of her worst physical and emotional wounds. Helen had the tremendous privilege of introducing Leslie to Jesus Christ. Through the years following, Helen nurtured and encouraged Leslie as God transformed her from a broken waif into a compassionate physician. That is exactly the kind of fruitfulness God wants to give as a blessing to every believer.

God has so much concern and compassion for us; he wants us to discover the joy and fulfillment that comes from reaching out and making a difference in other people's lives. When we start to walk with Jesus, he will help us discover our natural talents and motivated skill sets. Scripture teaches that he gives every believer at least one spiritual gift-- a special skill or strength which God will work through to have a profoundly powerful impact on people in your life. God has made us in his image. He gets great joy and pleasure from helping us discover all we were meant to be. And he lets his followers experience the same joy and pleasure. He is fully committed to helping you discover all your talents, skills, and strengths, and the best way you can apply them to people. In this way you will be able to experience the joy of seeing fruitful relationships blossoming with people you know and love.

So this is the abundant life. It's just a high level summary, of course. Scripture teaches us a lot more about it, and we will cover parts of it extensively later in this book. But I want you to get a taste of what God is offering to pour into your life as you walk with Jesus. He is opening all of the riches of His Kingdom to you and to me.

God offers us incredible spiritual resources for life. But he does not promise us a life without problems or difficulties. Please don't even hope for it. Jesus directs us, "In this world, you will have trouble." He goes on to promise his constant presence in life—in every trial, every tragedy, every circumstance, and he tells us, "Take heart! I have overcome the world." (John 16:33) When we walk with Jesus each day, he gives us supernatural peace and patience with whatever life throws at us. We have direct access to God through prayer 24 hours a day, seven days a week. We don't need a human intercessor because Jesus himself sits at the right hand of the Father and advocates for his followers.

Discussion Questions – Chapter 3

1) If you could be anybody in history or in a book, who would you want to be and why?

2) How would you define or describe "family"?

3) Do you have any childhood memories that spell family for you? Share one.

4) When you dream about the family you want to have, what comes to mind?

5) According to this chapter, what positive things can you expect in your life from having a growing relationship with Jesus? List as many as you can find.

6) If a friend asked you what your relationship with Jesus is like, what would you say?

7) Was there a part of the reading in this chapter that was particularly helpful for you, that made a connection in your mind, or that you disagree with? Share about that.

Growing with God

Chapter 4 – Overcoming Spiritual Obstacles

Some people think meeting Jesus is like winning the lottery or walking into a real life fairy tale. Once you trust Jesus, everything goes swimmingly in all areas of your life. "And they all lived happily after…" Hey, I have to admit; I would love to see that be the case. In my heart of hearts, all I really want is peace and prosperity - for me. However, the spiritual truth God brings us in the person of Jesus is not some Polly-Anna, get-rich-quick scheme, as some would have you believe.

When I was living in Boston, I used to get home late Sunday night from work, and I would flick on the TV. There at 11 PM I would find the Reverend Ike shouting out of my TV set. Reverend Ike was a skinny little black man in a $1,500 Italian suit. He would dance, he would prance, and he would strut across the stage like a banty rooster. He told his congregation, "God wants you to be rich. He wants you to be prosperous. He wants you to be successful! If you want a brand new green Cadillac, all you've got to do is ask God, and he'll give it to you. All you got to do is pray with faith and picture yourself driving down the street in that brand spankin' new green Cadillac, and it will be yours." He even quoted Scripture, "The Bible says, 'Seek ye first the kingdom of heaven and all of these **THINGS** will be added unto you.'" Not surprisingly, Reverend Ike had a lot of followers and a big TV audience. He was preaching a message people wanted to hear.

But the "Gospel of Prosperity" Reverend Ike preached is not the Gospel of Jesus or the Gospel of the Bible. There is simply no truth to the naive conviction that if a person is tight with God, he will be blessed with fame, fortune, and success. Jesus was left hanging in the hot sun from a cross after being nailed to it, not exactly a life of peace and prosperity for one who was sinless and perfect.

The truth of God demonstrated in the life and death of Jesus Christ is that God is not giving us a Gospel of peace and prosperity. Believers can be very close in their walk with God and still have to go through difficult experiences in this life.

DEALING WITH TOUGH TIMES

Karen, Reggie Morgan's sister, illustrates the point. Karen was raised in the same family as Reggie and in many ways they both experienced a lot of the same pain and dysfunction. Karen left home early and got married to Burr Griffin. It was as much to get out of her home as it was in hope the marriage would provide a new home she was yearning for. At the age of 22 she met Jesus and has enjoyed a close walk with him ever since, but it does not mean her life was problem free or pain free.

Karen and Burr have three children. Burr's job as a moving contractor involved a lot of time on the road and away from home. Often Karen struggled trying to raise the kids without much help from Burr. At one point their marriage went through a crisis that took several years to heal. As the oldest child of four children, Karen was often saddled with helping pick up the emotional fall-out of her two brothers and sister and for many years had her parents living off and on with her. Karen and Burr tried to develop the family farm into residential housing as an alternative to Burr's life on the road. Things went well until after they sold their first lot. Then the housing market collapsed, the savings and loan crisis drained billions from the U.S. economy and they lost both the farm and their family's finances.

Their three kids struggled with a typical array of teenage problems, such as alcohol, substance abuse, and other issues. After a year in college, Karen's daughter dropped out, moved home, got involved in a relationship, had a child out of wedlock and then had to deal with her son's father, who was more often than not in prison. At one point, Karen and Burr's finances got so bad they had to declare bankruptcy. Life is difficult. Life can be quite painful. Through all of these ups and downs, Karen kept walking with Jesus and drawing on his strength to get through the hard times. And Jesus got her through, but her most fervent wish was for her family to come to know and trust Jesus. Over the years, Karen shared her faith with both her family and friends. Her friends seemed much more receptive. Many eventually came to believe and follow Jesus. Her family did not.

About three years ago, the dam broke and her family started to join her in trusting Jesus. First her daughter Suzie accepted Christ and started to grow. The next spring her husband Burr finally trusted Jesus. Shortly after that, her oldest son Jack and his fiancé Bitsy both prayed and received Christ. Later that summer, her brother Reggie accepted Jesus and began his walk of faith. Wow! Karen was on a spiritual high! After all those years of praying and loving and hoping God would get through to them, almost her entire family came to faith over a couple of years.

And they lived happily ever after? No, actually, about 12 months after Burr accepted Christ, he was diagnosed with cancer of the throat and tongue. For the past year he has endured a slow crawl down into the pit of hell. He lost his hair, his voice, and his ability to eat and swallow. Over time the radiation and chemotherapy treatments poisoned him close to death. Then he had surgery. With the treatments done, it still may be six more months before he can chew and eat food on his own. He hasn't been able to work and they've had no income. They have struggled to save their home, put food on the table and pay for all the medicine and treatments. The process of caring for Burr, driving to hospitals in Boston almost every other day for months on end, and monitoring his condition and treatments has taken a tremendous toll on Karen. It's been an incredibly difficult ordeal for everyone.

Through it all, Burr and Karen's family and believing friends have pulled together and helped out in incredible ways. A close group of Christian friends come together every Monday night to pray for Burr and Karen and their needs. They have driven them back and forth to the hospital, stayed overnight with Karen when Burr couldn't come home, provided food and meals and financial support. They sat with Burr so Karen could get some rest. They helped with the intravenous feedings and other household needs. Karen sums up her experience of the last couple of years by saying, "It has been a difficult ordeal, but through it all, I finally have the kind of marriage and family life that I always hoped for and dreamed of and prayed for. Jesus has given us an incredible blessing through it all." Knowing Jesus, trusting Jesus, and following Jesus does not mean your life will be free from pain or trouble. It does not mean you will go through a set of experiences like Karen and Burr Griffin did, but there are no guarantees.

SPIRITUAL SETBACKS

In the beginning of your walk of faith, you may have no idea that spiritual setbacks are a possibility, no, more like a probability, in your walk with God. I start out trusting Jesus, faith is starting to make sense, and I feel God's presence in my life. I'm reading the Bible, I'm talking to another Christ follower and things are starting to click. Then... BOOM! Out of nowhere here comes a kick in the teeth. You get a body blow that knocks the wind out of you. Wow! How did that happen? I thought that once I was walking with Jesus, my life would be on Easy Street. Now here I am. I'm hurt, the wind is knocked out of me; I'm alone with my faith in Jesus with my doubts, with my Bible, with my friends, with my prayer life, but I'm alone! How could this happen? I need help!

This is actually good news. It's a sign of growth and health in your spiritual life. My friend Stu says growing with Jesus is a lot like the successive of stages of a rocket launch. You take off from the launch pad with this incredible sense of liftoff, of power, of progress, of God reaching down and taking hold of your life. You shower sparks everywhere, and you're off on a tear. Then the first booster rocket drops off. Oops! How did that happen? I thought it'd be like the first stage forever. Not! Learning to walk with Jesus is a process. It involves some tremendously positive and exhilarating experiences. It also involves times of trouble, doubt, failure, and fear. These are all normal stages in your growth and development. As C.S. Lewis put it so succinctly, "God whispers to us in our pleasures, speaks to us in our conscience, but shouts in our pains: it is his megaphone to rouse a deaf world."

So what causes us to hit Stage 2, the stage where our initial enthusiasm for walking with Jesus is brought up short by a painful kick in the teeth? The first cause of this type of spiritual setback is the struggle with our old human nature. When I became a believer, I was thrilled that I had Jesus in my life. I knew I was connected in a personal relationship with God through Jesus. I prayed regularly. I would talk to God and tell him how I was feeling and I'd ask for wisdom and guidance, or I would just pour out my heart to him. I didn't know about the Bible. The only person I knew who knew Jesus was hundreds of miles away and out of touch. So I was alone in this world with the Holy Spirit, Jesus, and God, the Father.

Growing with God

While I wanted to become a new person in Christ and I knew he was working in my life, I still had a lot of problems from my old life. Sexual promiscuity, lying, and stealing were still major issues God had yet to clean up in my life. Each of these problems had negative consequences I had to grapple with. The Bible describes what I experienced as the struggle between the old man (the person I was before Jesus) and the new man (my new nature in Christ with the Holy Spirit living inside of me transforming me to become like Jesus). In the book of Galatians, the Apostle Paul says that before Christ we were like slaves to our old nature—this caused us to indulge in all kinds of unhealthy things, which harmed us and offended God. But now that we have been set free in Christ—he's made us new people—"Therefore, if anyone is in Christ, he is a new creation; the old has gone, the new has come!" (2 Cor 5:17)

While Christ sets us free from slavery to our old self, we still must learn to walk in the Spirit. (Galatians 5:16-26) We need to become familiar with the new person Christ is making us to be. And that's a process. There are times when we fall back into the old habits, and then the stuff hits the fan. But we simply need to turn back to God, confess our failure, and we can be cleaned up and forgiven. Yes, in some ways, the beginnings of the journey of faith are two steps forward, one step back.

Eventually, hindsight will show you the progress you are making. I look back after years of following Christ and I see the battle – and that Jesus is winning the war between my old nature and my new nature. But it takes time. Even the Apostle Paul, after many years of following Jesus, complained about his continued failings. "I do not understand what I do. For what I want to do, I do not do, but what I hate, I do….for I have the desire to do good, but I cannot carry it out. For what I do is not the good I want to do; no, the evil I do not want to do—this I keep on doing." (Romans 7:15-20) Paul explains in Chapter 8 of the book of Romans, that even though this battle inside of us between our old nature and our new nature goes on for a lifetime, Jesus will gradually win the battle. By the time we leave this life and join Jesus in eternity, he will have transformed each of us so that we become like him. Wow!

HANDLING SPIRITUAL ATTACK

There is a second source of spiritual struggle and setbacks. It is not from anything within ourselves, nor is it caused by any source we can control. This source of spiritual setbacks often causes us to doubt our faith or the reality of God. How do we know Jesus is a historic person or that the Bible is trustworthy? Or we feel shame and guilt over past actions even though we have asked forgiveness. Perhaps we suffer from a poor self-image, doubt, fear, and anxiety over things in our daily life.

When you struggle with feelings and thoughts like this, don't worry. You may feel like you are falling out of your relationship with Jesus—but nothing could be further from the truth. Nothing has changed in your walk with God. What you are experiencing are the attacks of God's great enemy, Satan himself. "What? You don't expect me to believe in the devil, do you? You can't really believe the red guy with the forked tail and the horns on his head are real?"

Actually, I do. A recent national poll found that 80% of Americans believe in angels—beings with positive intent. Satan is simply a fallen angel – who has negative intent. Scripture says he was God's most important angel until he rebelled against God's leadership and got tossed out of heaven with his followers. Ever since Satan has been trying to attack and undermine God's work on earth in finding and rescuing every person on earth back into a restored relationship with the Father and with the forever family. (Revelation 12:7-9) The problem of evil, which is well known to all, is the problem of Satan prowling the earth wanting to lead the world astray.

As a new believer, you are likely to come under attack from Satan. Your position as an heir in God's family is secure. There is nothing Satan can do to undermine your salvation and your adoption into the forever family. Satan's strategies are threefold: he sets out to steal, to kill, and to destroy. If he gets you in his sights, he will try to destroy your faith. *The Screwtape Letters* by C.S. Lewis is perhaps the best introductory explanation of Satan for new believers. It's well worth a read.

How can we handle the devil? First be prepared for his periodic attacks. Second, realize that Satan has limited power. Jesus has already defeated Satan and his power over us—death—by Jesus' death on the cross and His resurrection.

(Colossians 2:13-15) As believers, all we have to do to overcome Satan's attack is to stand firm and resist him. "Resist the devil and he will flee from you! Come near to God and he will come near to you." (James 4:7-8)

LIFE HAPPENS

The last source of difficulty in the Christian life is not from problems within us or from spiritual attacks from agents of evil in the world. These trials simply come from the circumstances of life itself. As psychologist Scott Peck has so accurately observed, "Life is difficult." There are many things that happen in life, in which no blame or fault is due to the person who whom it happens. The terrorist attacks, which killed over 3,000 Americans on September 11, 2001, were not the fault of any of the innocent victims in the airplanes, in the World Trade Center, or in the Pentagon. Those who died or who were injured were not guiltier than those who didn't die that day.

Jesus describes a similar incident in Luke 13:1-5. He was asked if those involved in a vicious political killing were guilty of sin. Jesus answered, "Do you think those Galatians were worst sinners than all the other Galatians because they suffered this way? I tell you no! But unless you repent, you too will all perish. Or those 18 who died when the tower in Salome fell on them—do you think they were guiltier than all the others living in Jerusalem? I tell you, no!"

Circumstances can toss some of the most life-threatening, and life-changing challenges your way. If you turn to God and rely on his strength and wisdom to get you through these body blows, God can use them for good in your life. Romans 8:28 says that God will work all things for good in your life if you are walking with him. A friend of mine, reflecting on that passage, made the observation that the challenges of life can either build your character or make you bitter—depending on how you react to them.

This is vividly illustrated in the life of Donny McClure who we met in *Exploring God without Getting Religious*. Donny was getting along nicely in his life when one afternoon he was riding his Harley Davidson motorcycle home from work. Another driver failed to see him and pulled out into the road just as Donny came past the intersection. Donny and his bike were shattered. The accident almost killed him. He had broken bones all over his body. McClure spent the next two years in the hospital and rehabilitation. He lost his foot and the lower portion of his leg. He suffered from a variety of internal infections that led to depression and ended up living in a constant haze of pain and drugs....unable to heal; unable to move on.

Two years after the accident Donny told me, "I'm 40 years old and my entire life as I have known it has been destroyed. I have no idea what the future holds. I've often contemplated suicide. Only my faith and my daily relationship with Jesus have kept me sane through all of this. I simply don't know how I would have survived without his help." Because of his faith in Christ, today Donny is well on his way to building a new life. He's learned to accept and deal with his physical limitations and is now back working in a professional career and enjoying a lot of satisfaction in his life.

When you start to walk with God, use the good times to invest in a growing relationship. Discover the abundant life Jesus promises. Focus on learning good spiritual disciplines so your walk with God becomes strong and resilient. Difficult times will come. They may result from inner struggles with your old nature or sin habits left over from your days before Christ. You may get an unexpected kick in the teeth from Satan and his low-life pals. It may just be one of the circumstances of life that undermines your circumstances.

If you learn to walk with Jesus each day, he can transform even the cruelest tragedy into a source of new peace and health and character in your life. He is with you and helps you endure and overcome the worst that life can throw at you. The Bible tells us to rejoice in our sufferings because "we know that suffering produces perseverance; perseverance produces character; and character produces hope. Hope does not disappoint us because God has poured out his love into our hearts by the Holy Spirit, whom he has given us." (Romans 5:3-5)

Discussion Questions – Chapter 4

1) Tell the group about your favorite bedtime story as a child. Why that one?

2) Was there a time in your life when you thought the Christian life was just like a fairy tale? Once the prince rode in on his white horse, everything would go swimmingly – forever and ever? Share about that.

3) When did you first discover that you could have faith in God and still have hard things to deal with?

4) As you look back over your relationship with Jesus, can you see rough patches Jesus helped you to get through? Describe one.

5) When you are under spiritual attack, what are some constructive ways to deal with tough circumstances?

6) How might you use what you learned in this chapter to change your life in the coming week?

Growing with God

Chapter 5 – Creating an Environment for Growth

BROWNIE POINTS FOR HEAVEN?

So exactly how do you go about getting this abundant life? When I was a child, the supermarket where my mom shopped, would give out free Green Stamps. With every $10 worth of purchases, you'd receive 10 points in stamps. Some of the gas stations offered free Green Stamps with every fill-up. Eventually, in the rush to compete for shopper loyalty, retailers offered double or triple Green Stamps. When you accumulated enough points, you could go to the Green Stamp Store or use their catalog to redeem the points for a wide variety of household goods. Sheets, coffee pots, or electronic marvels like a transistor radio – all these could be yours for a stash of Green Stamps!

The more modern version of the "earn as you go scheme" is airline frequent flyer miles. If you accumulate 10,000 miles you can get a free upgrade to first class. 25,000 miles will get you a free ticket anywhere in the U.S. For 50,000 miles you can fly to Europe. When these schemes first came out, I watched the behavior of fellow corporate managers and executives and concluded these programs really work. Not only would employees steer all their travel to the airline they had the most miles with, when special promotions were offered (fly six flight legs between now and March 1 and win two free first class tickets), they suddenly had urgent business needs in the field that required them to fly to six cities before March 1!

Is this how you tap into the benefits that Jesus offers his followers? By earning points? By going to church with a certain frequency? Or by doing good deeds for others, praying often, or studying the Bible? Absolutely not! Just like the gracious offer of forgiveness and a new restored relationship with God through

Jesus, the abundant life is a free gift. Scripture tells us, "It is by God's grace you have been saved by faith. It is not the result of your own efforts, but God's gift so that no one can boast about it." (Ephesians 2:8) Our relationship with God is a free gift. Our adoption into the Father's eternal family is a free gift. The forgiveness of our past mistakes and our future mistakes is a free gift. Why would God require us to earn a lot of spiritual "brownie points" to obtain and access all the benefits of life in Christ?

While salvation is a free gift and the abundant life is a free gift there is one little catch. You can't **_do_** anything to earn either, but Jesus plainly teaches there are spiritual disciplines you can **_learn_** that will allow you to experience "life in abundance" rather than just drifting through life as in the past. Perhaps a word picture can illustrate what I mean.

Christmas is coming – what if I gave you a wonderfully exquisite chess set as a present? The pieces are 6" tall and hand carved from ivory by craftsman in Thailand. The chessboard is inlaid with mahogany, ebony, and silver— it's a set worth tens of thousands of dollars, but I give it to you for free. It's a free gift - but to enjoy the full potential of the gift, you will have to learn to play chess, and you will actually have to play chess to reap the all of the benefits of the free gift.

The abundant life Jesus gives to all believers works the same way. It's worth a fortune, but it's a free gift. It's a free gift, but if you never learn to use it, it benefits you very little. If you wanted to learn how to use your chess set, you would practice, get some lessons from a mentor, read, learn some plays and strategies, study and most of all, you'd practice by playing with others. But what would happen if instead of learning to use the gift, you simply thought about it occasionally as you drove to work? How much chess would you be able to play if that's all you invested in the process?

Yet that is about all the time and effort many believers invest in discovering the abundant life Jesus offers his followers. They pick up the Bible and read it once in awhile. If they get into a crisis, they try to pray and ask God for help. They occasionally go to a Christian concert, to church, or they plan to hang out with some other believers. Then it comes as a big surprise when they discover their walk with Jesus is pretty weak and anemic.

Jim Petersen describes how many believers end up completely passive and ineffective as far as their faith impact goes. He describes them as folks who are "sitting out the game of life in the bleachers." "Many of us feel so inadequate and unprepared that we simply consider ourselves unqualified to share our spiritual lives with others. We say, 'I have nothing to offer. My own life is in disarray. My marriage is in trouble. I'm worried about my kids. Financially we are barely making ends meet….my relationship with Christ isn't exactly transforming my life. What do I have that anyone else would want?'"[4]

JESUS' TEACHING ON FRUITFULNESS

Jesus often used agricultural illustrations to teach spiritual principles. One day he told his disciples this story. "A farmer went out to sow his seed. As he was scattering the seed, some fell along the path, and the birds came and ate it up. Some fell on rocky places, where it did not have much soil. It sprang up quickly, because the soil was shallow. But when the sun came up, the plants were scorched, and they withered because they had no root. Other seed fell among thorns, which grew up and choked the plants. Still other seed fell on good soil, where it produced a crop - a hundred, sixty, or thirty times what was sown."

His disciples asked what the parable meant and he said it was a picture of the spiritual health of those who meet Jesus. "When anyone hears the message about the kingdom and does not understand it, the evil one comes and snatches away what was sown in his heart. This is the seed sown along the path. The one who received the seed that fell on rocky places is the man who hears the word and at once receives it with joy. But since he has no root, he lasts only a short time. When trouble or persecution comes because of the word, he quickly falls away. The one who received the seed that fell among the thorns is the man who hears the word, but the worries of this life and the deceitfulness of wealth choke it, making it unfruitful. But the one who received the seed that fell on good soil is the man who hears the word and understands it. He produces a crop, yielding 100, 60, or 30 times what was sown." (Matt 13:3-8, 19-23)

Jesus wants each of us to live fruitful lives. He says that when we bear spiritual fruit it brings glory to God and shows we are his disciples. (John 15) As we learn to create a healthy environment for our spiritual growth, we can become like the soil that produces a hundred fold over what was sown. We will experience the joys and blessings of the abundant life in our own life, and we will have an impact the people in our world.

Plants in a garden need fertile soil, the right nutrients, good drainage, plenty of sunlight, room for growing strong roots, and regular watering. Your spiritual life is similar – a healthy environment with the right disciplines can make a big difference in the outcome. When a gardener wants to see what he needs to do have a more fruitful harvest, he does a soil test. The soil test determines where you are—is it the right pH, too alkaline, too acidic, and does it have the right levels of phosphorus, potassium, manganese, and calcium necessary for healthy plant growth? Then the successful gardener blends in lime, wood ash, leaf compost, chicken manure, or various chemical fertilizers in the right amounts to ensure the healthy and strong growth of this year's plants.

Learning the spiritual disciplines Jesus recommends to his followers has the same effect of multiplying the fruitfulness of our lives. Scripture teaches that you will reap what you sow. (2 Cor 9:6) If you learn the disciplines that lead to a healthy spiritual environment, you will reap a rich harvest of life abundant in your sojourn on earth. My hope and prayer are that you will be open to learn from what God has taught more mature believers through years of following Jesus. As I share these principles for spiritual health, I hope you will take them to Jesus and let him apply them to your life.

IT'S A RELATIONSHIP, NOT RULES!

What I want to share are some principles I've learned from God, from Scripture, and from other believers over the years. But please do not think that these are a set of rules, a religious recipe you must live your life by. Growing a healthy spiritual walk with God is not about rules or religion, although there are many who will try to convince you that is what you should do. A healthy spiritual life doesn't come from trying to keep a list of spiritual do's and don'ts. Many people fall into the trap of legalism, and it leaves them slaves to a religious system instead of helping them discover the abundant life Jesus wants us to have. Always remember God wants to grow a *relationship* with you—he doesn't want to enslave you to a set of rules or to a checklist of religious behaviors.

Growing with God

A man we will call Lenny was raised in a religious home. When he was in the Navy, he made a personal commitment to walk with Jesus. Back home he got involved in a Christian church that taught a brand of faith driven by an external devotion to rules and regulations. Lenny was a faithful practitioner—he didn't drink, he didn't dance, he didn't go to movies. He went to church anytime it was open, and he wore his best suit and tie. In the eyes of that church, he was a pillar of faith and an outstanding example of a Christian man. But keeping all those rules and regulations didn't help him grow in his walk with God, and it didn't promote spiritual fruitfulness in his heart—where it counts.

Eventually his family and marriage began to crumble and fall apart. The rules in his church said he was fine even though he didn't feel fine. He ended up sleeping with the teenage girl next door, but he was still in church every Sunday. His kids got in trouble, dropping out of school, living with troubled women, caught up with alcohol and drug addiction. Several even ended up in jail— children raised in a "loving Christian home." Now his marriage has collapsed, and he's working his way through a painful divorce. His life is so bad that he often contemplates suicide as the only solution left for him.

How could this happen to someone who knows Jesus? Lenny made the mistake of buying into a set of rules governing behaviors instead of developing his relationship with Jesus. He was deceived in thinking that external measures of performance are what matter to God, when in fact God cares about the condition of our hearts. Jesus tells his followers it doesn't matter what practices you keep on the outside because your true self flows outward from what's happening in your heart (Mark 7:14-19). Guard your heart, let Jesus fill your heart with his presence and values and your heart will shape and correct your outward behavior.

God challenged the human desire for a list of "do's and don'ts" long ago when his prophet Samuel said, "The Lord does not look at the things man looks at. Man looks at the outward appearance, but the Lord looks at the heart." (1 Samuel 16:7) Jesus warned the religious leaders of his day of this same error when he said, "Woe to you, you teachers of the Law and Pharisees, you hypocrites! You are like the white washed tombs, which look beautiful on the outside, but inside are full of dead men's bones and everything unclean. In the same way, on the outside you appear to people as righteous, but on the inside you are full of hypocrisy and wickedness." (Matthew 23:27-28)

TWO DISCIPLINES FOR SPIRITUAL GROWTH

Well then, if rules, religious regulations, and "do's and don'ts" are not the healthy way to develop a spiritual relationship with God, what are we supposed to do? It's actually quite simple. Jesus gives us two overarching principles, which he says summarizes all of God's direction for us contained in the Bible (66 books and 1,300 pages). He boils down God's instructions for spiritual growth for his followers into two simple principles:

- "Love the Lord your God with all your heart, with all your soul, and with all your mind."
- "Love your neighbor as yourself." (Matthew 22:37-40)

Knowing God comes via your relationship with Jesus. It's not about religion or rules, it's about a relationship. Small wonder then that God sums up all that is required in a healthy spiritual life by focusing on our relationship with Him and our relationships with other people. When we trust Jesus and start walking with him into a relationship with God, the Holy Spirit comes and lives inside of us. (Galatians 2:20-21) Jesus said he would send the Holy Spirit to us to speak the truth to us (John 16:13), to live with us (John 14:17), to be in us (John 14:17), to remind us of everything Jesus has said (John 14:26), to teach us everything we need (John 14:26), to testify about Jesus (John 15:26), and to take God's wisdom from Jesus and make it known to us (John 16:14).

Recognizing the power for spiritual living we've been given in the gift of the Holy Spirit, why would we ever need a list of do's and don'ts to govern our behavior? If we could have the spirit of the living God within us, why would we want to settle for a narrow-minded religious rulebook to teach us and guide us? Our lives and experiences are far too complex to be managed by a single set of rules.

God wants us to learn to walk with the Holy Spirit each day, to hear his voice speaking to us, to learn how to trust God with the decisions and issues that face us each day. He knows however, it is all too easy for us to veer off the road too far to the left or to the right and get into trouble. So he gives us two sets of spiritual disciplines to protect us. Each of these disciplines plays a role in keeping our lives where the Holy Spirit can effectively guide us.

These disciplines remind me of trying to teach a child to bowl. The object, for the young bowler, is to learn to guide the ball down the alley so that it hits the pins at the end. For beginners, the toughest trick to master is to get the ball to stay out of the gutters on either side long enough to get anywhere near the pins. A helpful technique used by those who train beginning bowlers is to put inflatable bumpers in each gutter, so the ball can get down the alley without falling out of play on either side.

These two sets of spiritual disciplines serve the same purpose in our lives as we learn to walk by the Spirit with God. I call these disciplines that Jesus introduced our *personal disciplines* and our *relational disciplines*. Learning to love God with all our heart, mind and soul is the objective of the three personal disciplines that I'm going to share with you. Learning to love your neighbor as yourself is the objective of the three relational disciplines. Together these sets of disciplines will serve as bumpers on the bowling alley of your spiritual life. They will keep you from veering off into extremes on either side of the path God would have you to take. They will serve to guide you and protect you so the Holy Spirit can lead you every day and teach you what Jesus has for you in life. These disciplines are principles all believers share in common, even though specific applications under the guidance of God's Spirit will be unique for each person.

THE SPIRITUAL DISCIPLINES

The *personal disciplines* God gives us to help us learn to walk in the Spirit are:
1. Making your relationship with God a high priority
2. Learning to talk to and listen to God
3. Learning how to learn from God

The *relational disciplines* include:
1. Being part of an accountable community
2. Learning to share with those who are needy
3. Learning to share your faith with those who are spiritually hungry

Both the personal and relational disciplines are necessary to ensure your healthy spiritual development. Many make the mistake of having one but not the other kind of discipline and reap a world of trouble. Today we often hear of ministers or other Christian leaders who fall into disgrace from some moral or ethical failure. When you read the details of each case, you almost always find someone who has a strong set of personal disciplines, but no relational disciplines in their walk with God. Their theology may have been excellent, but the lack of Biblical community undermined their entire faith walk.

Many new believers never miss the opportunity to be with other Christ followers to talk and share about their faith in peopled settings. In a sense they live their faith vicariously through other people by focusing only on the relational disciplines. But these extraverted believers never take the time to meet alone with God and to learn to hear his voice, draw on his power, and accept his leadership and direction in their personal life. The result is a life Jesus described as being like a plant with shallow roots that never develop. When the time of testing comes, they cannot endure. When tragedy strikes, when a loved one is lost, when they lose their job, when calamity strikes—they discover they have failed to build a strong connection to Jesus, and they lack the spiritual stamina to weather the storms and testing of life.

So both the personal disciplines and the relational disciplines are necessary to grow a healthy spiritual life. As you learn to develop these in your own life, you will find your faith and your relationship with God deepen every day. When the storms of life hit, you will find that you are able to endure and access God's strength. You will have the spiritual resources to get through tough times. You will find your life fruitful in terms of being able to be a positive influence on those around you in your life.

Over the course of the next six chapters we will discuss each discipline and take a look at how you can claim these and develop them so that you too might experience all the riches and blessings God has for you in the abundant life.

<u>Discussion Questions – Chapter 5</u>

1) Describe learning a new skill, sport, or game as a child. What did it take to become good at this activity?

2) Pick a favorite relationship from your elementary or teen years and tell us about it. What made it special?

3) How do you feel about the fruitfulness of your current spiritual life? Are there areas you'd like to improve on?

4) Have you ever thought faith was about keeping a list of do's and don'ts? What kinds of things were on these lists?

5) If faith is about a relationship and not rules, how does that change our spiritual life?

6) What information in this chapter was new information for you?

7) Which of the two areas of spiritual discipline are better developed in your life – the personal disciplines or the relational disciplines?

Growing with God

Chapter 6 – The Power of Priorities

BEGIN WITH THE END IN MIND

Lou and Tara Fox were children of the 70's. Both grew up in middle class
American families. Both got off track fairly early in adolescence. Lou's Dad was
in the Navy, so he lived in a succession of places, never spending more than two
years in any one school. San Diego, Pensacola, Norfolk, Virginia…town after
town came and went during his childhood. Finally, he just stopped trying to make
friends and cope with having to leave them. He turned to alcohol and drugs for
solace. Lou was an alcoholic before he was 20.

Tara grew up in the home of two driven and successful parents. Both her
mom and dad were career professionals who worked in finance and investments
and made a boatload of money. Tara was often ignored or left behind and was
finally was shipped off to a series of boarding schools. Her response to the
personal hurt and neglect she felt was to rebel. She aggressively investigated and
participated in every kind of trouble she could stir up. Eventually, alcohol and
drugs claimed the major share of her attention. By her second year of college,
Tara was a full-blown pill addict and alcoholic.

Alcohol and drug addiction can cause a great deal of trouble when one
tries to adjust to the real world of holding down a job. It's no great surprise then
that Lou and Tara had difficulties with work. Lou realized he needed to get sober
if he was going to survive, so he joined Alcoholics Anonymous. Tara was
introduced to Jesus by a college roommate and eventually made a commitment to
follow Him. She too joined AA and ALANON and began the long climb to
sobriety, sanity, and healing in her life. That's where Lou and Tara met, at an AA
group which gathered outside of Framingham, MA. They dated and eventually
married.

Under the influence of her faith walk with Jesus, Tara slowly began to get direction for her life. A new maturity and stability infused their marriage relationship. They had two lovely daughters, and Lou eventually decided to commit his life to Jesus as well. As Tara and Lou matured in their faith, their professional careers became increasingly successful. After ten years of marriage, they finally had the financial ability to move to a wonderful suburb and build their dream house. Set on a two-acre lawn surrounded by eight acres of woods, the home was large, rambling, and luxurious. Even before they moved in, they sank every cent they had (and a lot of money they borrowed) in making this a "Better Homes and Gardens" showcase home. A professional interior decorator made sure every room was decorated in the finest ornamentations.

A beautiful home in a beautiful neighborhood, great jobs and two wonderful kids—what happened to their spiritual lives as they were enjoying all this success? Truthfully, not much. They were way too busy to invest much time in their relationship with God. They were so busy working to pay for the dream-house, they hardly had time for each other or the kids, let alone to set time aside to be with God. Their mortgage was enormous. The bills for the furniture, the decorating, and the landscaping, were incredible. Lou and Tara had to work extremely long hours to try and earn enough to pay for the dream. Now that they had it, it seemed that they had little time to enjoy it. But they got to church once in awhile, and they put both their girls in a Christian day school. But in general, life was too flat-out hectic to invest much in their relationship with God or with each other.

Let me make a small aside to the narrative. Too busy is a choice. While many protest it's a circumstance beyond their control. This is simply not true. It's a choice you make and it's a choice you can unmake – up until the disaster hits. Then it may be too late.

Here was a family who had everything, and then some! All the grace, love, and power of Jesus in their lives to lead and guide them were theirs. The Foxes had everything, yet this story ends in tragedy. After years of stress and strain and long hours at work, Lou finally cracked. He started an affair with a woman at work, and shortly after he left home and moved in with his new companion. He began to drink again and slid back down into the pit of alcoholism and despair. Tara reacted by working harder and trying to compensate with the children, but she too eventually snapped under the pressure and was often drunk by 8 AM in the morning.

The little girls have never recovered. They cry, are depressed, and often appear catatonic as they are shifted between grandparents, daycare, and school. They cannot understand what happened to Daddy and their family and their home. And the dream house? Eventually, after the marriage collapsed, that was lost as well. Proverbs 14:12 says, "There is a way that seems right to a man, but in the end it leads to death." Later in this same chapter we read, "The fear of the Lord is a fountain of life turning a man from the snares of death." (Proverbs 14:27)

Spiritually, when we walk with Jesus, we are given unlimited access to enormous wealth and riches. Yet the Foxes demonstrate how we can be given all of those riches and still end up squandering them—finishing as bankrupt paupers. All believers are given the gifts of the abundant life. But only those who unwrap the gifts and use them experience the blessing God intends for us in this life. The first spiritual discipline we need to learn as we walk with Jesus is to make our relationship with him a top priority. Making sure that we regularly and consistently set aside high quality time for our relationship with God is the primary difference between discovering and living a life full of spiritual blessings and creating an unmitigated disaster out of the life we have been given.

MAKE YOUR RELATIONSHIP WITH GOD A TOP PRIORITY

The power of priorities is probably one of the most important lessons God has taught me as I have walked with him over the past 30 years. It's not what I **think** about God that changes my life, it's not how I **feel** about God's love for me in Jesus that changes my life, it's not a set of cognitive **beliefs** I agree with that changes my life. It's when I let God change my priorities - then I begin to see him making a profound and dramatic difference in shaping how I live.

What do I mean by "priorities"? The word *priorities* is just another way of saying, "what gets done first? What gets done if nothing else gets done?" When we set priorities in our life, we answer questions like these:

- What's really essential to my life?
- What or who is my faith based on?
- What will I do first?

- What do I want to do best?
- Whom am I trying to impress?

Priorities are critical because they shape the outcome of our lives. Though rarely mentioned and seldom debated in our world, priorities make all the difference in the results of people's lives. Lots of people start out life with significant advantages. They may have health, physical strength, intelligence, skills, education, and passion. But so many who have an abundance of personal assets seem to end up living such poor lives. With all the advantages, they finish their lives having lived badly.

Others with much more modest talents and assets, even many people with significant challenges and obstacles to overcome, end up living lives that are remarkable for their success and fulfillment. How is it that people who start the race of life with much less, often seems to finish living lives marked by abundance and joy? The answer is priorities. One's priorities and not one's initial assets in life, determine the end result of a life. Priorities determine what actually gets taken care of in a world with way too many needs and demands and not enough time and resources.

If you spend more time on Facebook, Twitter, or clever apps on your smart phone than you do getting to know God; it is going to have a major impact on your life. Each priority, each choice you make on where to focus your attention, is going to determine the outcomes of your life.

Let's look at Jesus' summation of the principles for following God and enjoying the abundant life. First he tells us, "Love the Lord, your God, with all of your heart, and with all of your soul, and with all of your mind." Does this sound like a casual commitment to you? I know some believers who honestly think all they need to do to invest in a relationship with God is to go to church once in a while. Or to read some Bible passages when you have the chance, or to occasionally shoot up a prayer to God, especially when you cannot find a parking space! And they wonder why God never seems to be doing much in their life. Or why they can't see where the "spiritual blessing" enters the equation.

In an article for *Books and Culture*, Mark Buchanan describes how many believers often approach our faith. "We want a personal God who doesn't ask much personally. We want mystery, but in a controlled, non-disruptive way. We want a faith that is fulfilling, practical, earthy, tolerant, transcendent, fun, empowering, and morally serious without being morally demanding, a faith that restores wonder and deepens intimacy, and we want it not to cost too much or to take up a lot of time."

Dave Burchett is an Emmy award-winning television sports director for Fox Sports, ESPN, and NBC. He is also a committed follower of Jesus. He shares his own struggles with priorities and making enough time for his relationship with God. "Just like the people in beer and investment commercials on TV, we Christians want it all. Time is a currency. You spend it on what is important to you. One of my core beliefs is that investment of your time (over a long period) is a pretty accurate indicator of your priorities and actual loves. If I claim to love my children but make little or no time for them, then my claim rings hollow."

Burchett goes on to describe research that indicates most American believers spend an average of seven times more hours each week watching television than they do in spiritual pursuits. They spend more time surfing the Internet than they do conversing with God in prayer, and they spend more time studying the sports pages than they do studying the Bible. Burchett's response, "Busted! I am truly embarrassed to report that I can name every starter from the 1961 Cincinnati Reds but would struggle to name all twelve of Jesus' disciples. You make time for what is important."[5]

Don't get me wrong on this—God is not against careers, hobbies, or other activities. God is not anti-success or anti-career, but I believe he is pro-balance. We need to seek the Lord so we can develop the right balance in our lives. When we take the time to make our relationship with God our top priority, then our relationships with our spouse and kids (if we are married and have family) will rise to their proper place. Over time, God will help us work out the other commitments in our lives in a way that makes a healthy whole. Jesus' life showed this kind of healthy balance. He often attended wedding feasts and parties. He spent time hanging out with his disciples—they even went on vacation together. But he balanced those times with times spent alone in prayer and reflection. So many Americans live lives that are totally out of balance and so do many Americans who know and love Jesus.

One helpful tool to allow you to get a handle on your priorities is to keep a time log. Simply get a sheet of paper and divide it into 15-minute blocks for all of your waking hours of the day. Then track how you actually invest your time for a couple of weeks or a month. You may be surprised. Find out how much time you are actually setting aside for God or for your relationship with your spouse or with your kids or with other friends or people God has put in your life. Or go back and look at your calendar for the past few months. What were the big time commitments you invested your life in? Your checkbook can tell you something about your priorities. How are you investing your money? In what kinds of priorities and activities are you spending your scarce resources? How do these measures fit with the priorities and outcomes you want for your life?

THE PARADOX PRINCIPLE

There is a paradox in living a spiritual life. Jesus describes it this way, "The man who loves his life will lose it, while the man who hates his life in this world will keep it for eternity." (John 12:23-26) We find ourselves so busy, preoccupied, and filled with strife and anxiety about so many things. "How could I possibly squeeze more time into my already too busy life to make time for my relationship with God?" we ask. The reality is that many of us lead lives that are so busy and so full but in the end, all they produce is emptiness. We labor and strive but do so in vain. We never find the peace and satisfaction and fulfillment we are seeking through all our striving and efforts.

Jesus explained to his followers that the power for successful living comes directly from being connected to the source of life and power – Jesus himself. He said, "I am the vine; you are the branches. If a man remains in me and I in him, he will bear much fruit; apart from me you can do nothing. If anyone does not remain in me, he is like a branch that is thrown away and withers; such branches are picked up, thrown into the fire and burned. If you remain in me and my words remain in you, ask whatever you wish, and it will be given you. This is to my Father's glory, that you bear much fruit, showing yourselves to be my disciples." (John 15:5-8)

The only way our lives can bear the fruit we desire is to be connected to Jesus; to focus on him and to grow in our relationship with him each day. That means we are going to have to sacrifice some of the effort and striving which now consume our lives. The result of cutting out a lot of that empty stuff and learning to "remain in Jesus" is that we will begin to see the fruit in our personal lives and in the lives of those around us that we were hoping to find through all of our striving.

"Jesus did many miraculous signs in the presence of his disciples…these are written so that you may believe that Jesus is the Christ, the Son of God, and that by believing you may have life in his name." (John 20:30-31) Do you want to have God do miraculous signs in your life? If so, you're going to have to clear out some space for him. You're going to have to rearrange your priorities and make your relationship with God a top priority—one that gets enough time and one that gets enough quality time. The leftover time in your life will not do, if you want to have "life in His Name." The gift of abundant life is free to all who accept Jesus, but you have to make time to unwrap the gift and learn how to use it if you hope to have all the benefits in your life.

DON'T LEAD AN UNEXAMINED LIFE

Rebuilding your life in order to make your relationship with God a top priority will take time. It won't happen over night. If you're anything like me, I'm sure you will have failures along the way. But stick with it, and you will learn how to do it. My wife says learning a new habit takes 21 days. She's probably right, although I've gone through the 21 days a number of different times trying to give God quality time on a regular basis.

Some days I feel like Bill Murray in the movie, **Groundhog Day**. He plays the part of a TV weatherman who goes to Punxsutawney, PA, to broadcast the February 2 ceremony with the ground hog and his shadow. The weatherman has a serious attitude problem and as a result, he finds himself condemned to waking up every day at 6 AM and finding it is still February 2. Day after day he experiences the same relationships, the same events, and makes the same mistakes at the same time each day. Sometimes that's what my life feels like. Changing old habits is hard. Developing new habits is harder yet. But God is on our side with this one. If we really want to make time for a growing relationship with God, he will help us. All we have to do is to try and keep trying and to ask for his help, and he will provide what we lack so it becomes a reality. Pray and ask God to give you a hunger and thirst for time alone with him. He'll honor that prayer in your life, just as he has in mine.

As I look back over my life, I can see a lot of habits I haven't done a great job of changing. I still have tendencies toward being a workaholic. I don't exercise nearly as much as I should. I have a tendency to eat food out of emotional need rather than physical need. But my spiritual life is pretty healthy. God has really enabled me to desire to be with him and to work to make my relationship with him a top priority. Now, I find I really need and want time to reflect. I don't want to live an unexamined life and waste the one I've been given. I love getting up in the morning and spending time with God, reading his Word, talking to him, listening to him, and meditating on what he's teaching me about life. He helps me to process what's happening in my life, he shows me his perspectives on people and issues, corrects me when my attitude is wrong, helps me believe him for what he wants to do in my life and in the lives of people around me.

So how are you doing with making your relationship with God a top priority? Do you have regular time to cultivate your relationship each day, each week? Are you seeing God at work in your life, making changes and influencing the people around you? If you aren't seeing much spiritual fruit in your life, it may be because you haven't taken the time to invest in unwrapping the gift of abundant life. You do reap what you sow in spiritual growth. If you invest a little, you'll get a little. If you invest a bit more, you'll get a lot more.

My friend Stu is a new believer, having met Jesus about nine months ago. He discovered this principle in his own life as he started walking with Jesus. He told me, "You know, when I first met Christ I made time to talk with him in the morning and even on my commute to work. Everyday I set apart some time to read the Bible and to reflect on what I was learning. I've a lot of questions and doubts, but I found God quite willing to entertain them and help me learn more and grow more in my knowledge and understanding. Then things got really busy at work; my wife and daughter got the flu, and even my Mom who came to visit came down with a horrible cold. Next thing you know, I stopped making time for God. I just got too busy and things really started to go wrong."

"So I thought, 'I know. I'll just go to church on Sunday. I can invest an hour and make up all the time that I missed with God during the week on my own. Boy, was I ever wrong about that! Now I realize that I have to make time to invest in my relationship with Jesus if I am going to grow and see good fruit in my life. You can't just go to church and expect them to tell you what to do. You need personal time, one-on-one, with God yourself."

So take Stu's advice. Make time to grow with God. Don't look for an easy answer. Church is not a short cut, nor is it a substitute for your own personal relationship with God. The only way you can have a growing, fruitful relationship with God is if you make it a priority and invest your own quality time on a regular basis. Get to know God and grow in His grace.

Discussion Questions – Chapter 6

1) Thinking back to your childhood, describe your approach to Christmas gifts: did you try to find out what you were getting, wait patiently for Christmas Day, or what?

2) Do you agree or disagree with this statement & why? "Too busy is a choice."

3) How can we identify what our priorities actually are?

4) What kind of priorities does your checkbook show? How about your calendar?

5) When, where and how have you been most successful in spending time with God?

6) What could you stop doing in your life to free up more time for God?

7) Do you ever see spiritual fruit in your life? Explain your answer.

Growing with God

Chapter 7 – Talking with God

GOD WANTS TO BRING CHANGE

God is in the business of changing things. Is there anything in your life you wish you could change: A personality trait, a bad habit, a consequence of previous mistakes, a personal weakness, a broken relationship, or a negative circumstance? God is in the change business. He's in the business of transforming our lives from what they are or have been in the past, to something entirely new. Something much better. God does not simply want to fix the brokenness in our lives; he wants to make us into new creatures.

Spiritual growth is all about change—for the better. In Romans 12:2 we read, "Don't let the world around you squeeze you into its own mold, but let God re-make you so that your whole attitude of mind is changed. Thus you will prove in practice that the will of God is good, acceptable to him and perfect."[6]

Through our relationship with Jesus, God commits all of his love and power to help each of us to change—for the better. You may have trouble believing you can change. You may have had a lot of trouble trying to change on your own in the past. Like me, you may have suffered a lot of defeats or setbacks in your efforts to try and improve yourself and your circumstances by your own efforts. But God is now committing himself and all of his unlimited resources to help each of us change. His goal is that when we finally leave this life, we will "be like Jesus."

Do you want God to transform your life for the better? The most important thing you can do to facilitate that process is to learn to communicate effectively with God. Learning to talk and listen to the other person is the most important element in our human relationships. It's no different with God. When you think about your relationship with a friend, or with your marriage partner, or as a parent with a child, or as a child with your parent—all of these relationships are dependent on effective communication. What happens when there is a miscommunication or failure to communicate with your spouse? Mostly bad things and hurt feelings. The relationships in your life that provide the most support, encouragement, and personal growth are the relationships in which you enjoy the best communication. It's no different in your relationship with your Heavenly Father.

God cares about the circumstances and issues in our lives. There is nothing too big for his power, nor too small for his attention. He wants us to learn to talk with him and listen to him about all of these things. Janet Larsen, a 47-year-old dental hygienist, boarded a plane to Memphis to see her younger sister Debbie who was in the hospital in Louisiana. Debbie, 41, had suffered for seven years from a diseased liver and from kidney failure. Three years ago she had a liver transplant, which her body rejected. Without a successful transplant soon, the doctors put her life expectancy as a matter of months. As she settled into her seat, Janet prayed, "Please Lord, let me help give Debbie her life back."

Seated next to Janet Larson on Northwest Airlines Flight 1815 was Alan Van Meter. Alan's 25-year-old nephew, Mike Gibson, had been involved in a tragic accident the day before and lay brain dead on life support in a Springfield, Missouri hospital. The doctors told the family there was nothing left to do but harvest his organs and turn off the life support. The night before Van Meter had called the airline and gotten the last seat left on the plane, next to Janet Larsen, in order to go to Missouri to comfort his sister and her husband.

Alan sat quietly preparing for the emotional ordeal ahead. When he saw Janet studying an anatomical drawing, he started a conversation. As they both shared the reason for their trips, Alan suddenly said, "Hey, look we've got to do something about this!" In spite of the long odds of a compatible match, Janet's stunned skepticism, and the incredible time and logistic barriers—Alan was convinced they should try and get his nephew's liver for Janet's sister. He picked up the airline phone and went to work. After hours of calls, miraculous interventions, and a number of other far fetched "coincidences" the impossible became a reality. Two days later Debbie awoke with a new liver, donated by Alan's nephew, and a new lease on life. The transplant was accepted, and Debbie is well on her way to recovering from her 10-year nightmare of sickness and decline. The transplant has also made a huge difference in Janet's life. Seeing the miracle God worked with her one silent prayer has really opened her eyes to all that God wants to do in her life as she grows in her faith walk with Him.[7]

PRAYER IS A LEARNED SKILL

Prayer, learning to talk and to listen to God, is a critical skill to learn if you are going to have a growing spiritual life. Jesus talks about prayer to his followers in 40 different passages of the New Testament. He tells us to pray in a quiet place where we can have an intimate conversation with our Heavenly Father who loves us. He tells us to call him Daddy (Abba in the Aramaic). Expect him to listen and to respond in love. Don't babble or talk in funny religious language—God already knows what you need before you ask him, Jesus says and his heart is inclined towards you with love and compassion.

Jesus instructs his followers to pray in this way, "Our Father in heaven; may your holy name be honored; may your Kingdom come; may your will be done on earth as it is in heaven. Give us today the food we need. Forgive us the wrongs we have done, as we forgive the wrongs that others have done to us. Do not bring us to hard testing, but keep us safe from the Evil One."[8]

Jesus teaches us to ask God to align our hearts and minds, which are so easily distracted by all the things of this world, with his spiritual purposes and perspectives. We are to pray that God's will shall come to pass in our hearts and the lives of those around us—that's when we see the abundant life changing things for the better! We can ask him to provide for our physical needs and to help us forgive others—that we may be forgiven ourselves. Finally, we are instructed to pray for protection from both temptation (our own weaknesses) and from attacks by Satan (the Evil One).

Let me give you some pointers on environmental issues that affect your prayer. In order to find prayer an effective dialog between you and God, you will have to develop prayer habits that work for you. I like to set aside a half-hour at the beginning of every day to talk to God. I do it early in the morning, so I can get up before anyone else in the house is around to distract me. When my kids were in high school that meant I had to get up at 5 AM to beat them to the shower and still have that quiet block of time to talk with God. You need to find an environment without distractions. When my wife comes down to breakfast, she loves to switch on the radio and listen to the news and weather on NPR. But I really have trouble hearing God talk (or me either) with Nina Totenburg yakking in the background. So I carefully plan my schedule to avoid the audio competition. My friend Karl finds his home distracting, so he gets an early train into Chicago and goes into his office where he can have a time of uninterrupted conversation with the Lord.

I have a special chair I sit in when I talk to God and study His Word in the morning. It helps me to focus on the relationship because that place is set aside for that one purpose. When I commuted an hour to work, I would read the Bible before I left and for the first half hour on the road, I would have the radio off and I would pray. In another house, I found I could focus best by taking a walk around the various blocks in our neighborhood. That way, I got uninterrupted time alone with God and got some fresh air and exercise at the same time.

FOUR KINDS OF PRAYER

So what do I pray about? Basically, God wants you to talk to him about anything that's on your heart and mind. I had a mentor who divided the topic of his prayer life into four sections. **Adoration** is simply praising God for who he is, what he's doing in your life, what he's doing in the world, and what he's done in history, for his personality and his attributes. I often simply pray verses of Scripture about God I read in the Bible as a way of praising Him.

Confession is where we really get honest with God about what's going on in our life. It's not limited to asking forgiveness for some mistake we've made, although it includes that. We will all need to confess things that we've done or said that hurt other people, hurt ourselves, or hurt God. The Apostle John tells us, "If we claim to be without sin, we deceive ourselves and the truth is not in us." (1 John 1:8) John goes on to share the good news on the problem of screwing up, which I seem to need so often. "If we confess our sins, he is faithful and just and will forgive us our sins and purify us from all unrighteousness." (1 John 1:9)

Thanksgiving is the next category of prayer. While sometimes our lives seem to be like a glass—half full or half empty depending on how we look at it— we need to cultivate an attitude of gratefulness. "Gratitude is the key to a new attitude" is what my wife tells her elementary school students. I find this principle applies to me as well. So I want to focus some time on thanking God for all the good things that he's given me and put into my life. My families, my friends, my work, the beautiful spring sunshine, the softly falling snow flakes, the majesty of the stars at night, the wonderful sounds of birds singing that come through the window on balmy soft breezes. We need to learn to slow down, to see what good God has actually put into our lives and to learn to enjoy the beauty of each day and each person God fills our world with.

Request is the final category that you should include in your prayers. Here's where we ask God to change things in our world. "Give me a thirst to know you and to learn from you, Lord!" is one of my favorite requests. I pray regularly for my wife and family, for people whose needs and concerns I know about, often I pray silently for people I see as I drive or walk down the street. God wants to help us with all the little details of our lives. That includes finding a parking space. Jesus told his followers (in Matthew 6:19-34) that God provides food for the sparrows and clothes for the lilies of the field—what makes you think that he wouldn't want to provide for your needs as well?

When I was first married, my wife and I moved from California to Princeton, New Jersey in our 10-year old Ford Falcon in order to take a new job. Everything we owned fit into that small four-door sedan. My new job was entry level—I made minimum wage. When I sat down to figure out our bare minimum budget to pay for the apartment, food, and gas for the car, it came to $365 more per month than my take-home pay. After two weeks, the old Falcon broke down, and I had to take it to a service station for repair. I was a nervous wreck all day because I knew I only had $67 to my name, and the repair was sure to cost more than that. So Martie and I prayed and asked God to help get our car fixed.

That afternoon when I went to pick it up, I asked how much I owed. The mechanic said, "Nothing. Somebody already came by and paid the bill." What's even more amazing, the only two people we knew in Princeton were out of town that day! God loves to provide little miracles to meet our daily needs. It's vitally important to understand that God is committed to answering our prayers. Jesus says, "God will always give what is right to His people who cry to him night and day and he will not be slow to answer them." (Luke 18:7) God loves each of us, is attuned to our voice, and is listening everyday to hear our concerns and to respond with his love.

GOD WANTS TO HEAR FROM US

My daughters are both in college away from home. Yet, nothing thrills me more than to have them call me in the middle of the day to talk to me. My staff has strict instructions—it doesn't matter who I'm meeting with or who I'm on the phone with—when my girls call, they are to interrupt me and put them through. I don't care if I'm on a conference call with the President of the United States. If one of my girls calls, I put them on hold and talk to my little darling. It doesn't matter why they call—it could be a question about their course selection, or some financial need, or a thought about what they are doing this coming summer. It doesn't matter if the issue is large or small—I just love to hear their voice, and I'm so glad they bothered to call me. I'm honored by their request, and I want to do *anything* in my power to help them out. Anything!

God feels the same way when we stop and talk to Him. It just brightens his day to hear our voice. He is delighted to have the chance to help us. And unlike me, a human father, His power and love are unlimited. There is nothing beyond his ability to pull off for the children he loves. Now that doesn't mean God will give you anything you pray for. God always answers our prayers. He can answer "yes", he can answer "no", or he can answer "maybe later." Just because God doesn't immediately grant you what you ask for doesn't mean he hasn't answered your prayer. Scripture teaches us that God, like a loving heavenly father, will only give us those things that are truly good for us. Jesus put it this way, "Which of you if his son asks for bread, will give him a stone? Or if he asks for fish, will you give him a snake? If you then, though you are evil, know how to give good gifts to your children, how much more will your Father in heaven give good gifts to those who ask him?" (Matthew 7:9-11)

Sometimes our prayer requests involve things that aren't appropriate, nor are they in keeping with God's values and perspectives....and God answers "no". Other times things we request are right on target, but the timing is off. God will delay those answers until the time is right. Sometimes God says "yes", but the answer looks so different from the way we had envisioned it coming that it takes us awhile to figure out that he has indeed answered our prayer.

PRAYER IS DIALOG

Listening to God is even more important than learning to talk with God. God does want to have us pour out our heart, our thoughts, our feelings, and everything we are concerned about. Some believers never get past this, they simply vomit up all of their feelings when they meet with God and then they walk off—never having heard his gracious response to all of their babbling. These believers think that prayer is mostly a one-way conversation, sort of like a little kid on the department store Santa's knee, where they get to reel off their wish list for Christmas.

This monologue approach to prayer misses the most important part—hearing what God has to say to you. God is just overflowing with love, compassion, mercy, wisdom, guidance, and help that he wants to pour into your life in a very special, individual, and personal way. If you simply drop your load of woe and take off without listening, you never receive any of the precious love gifts the Father wants to give you.

So how do you learn to listen to God? Let me suggest several ways that you can learn to improve your listening skills (most of us, myself included, could use help with this) and discover all the wonderful things God wants to say to you. There are lots of ways to listen to God, but they all have one thing in common. Solitude is the key to hearing God's voice. Most of us lead busy, active lives. If we want to hear from God, we are going to have to learn to slow down and to listen to God. If you look at Jesus in the New Testament, he was always going off alone to a place where he could be still and quiet so he could talk to his heavenly Father. Psalm 46:10 says, "Be still and know that I am God." If you want to have God speak to you directly and personally, you will need to seek a place of solitude and quiet without distractions. This could be in your bedroom, the corner of the garage, in your car, in a public park, in the reading stacks of a library. But you need to get still, get quiet, and be able to focus your mind and your spirit on God and then wait patiently to hear what he has to say to you.

I often do this by sitting in my prayer chair clearing my mind, taking a pen and a clean pad of paper and asking God what he wants to say to me. I'm thinking he's going to tell me to move to Madison, Wisconsin, change careers, or go be a missionary in the Bongo Congo in Africa. I'm so focused on doing and the activities in my life that I simply don't get what God is all about. Instead of telling me to do something, he will often say, "I love you, Bruce. Trust me. Relax in my love. I will never leave you nor abandon you."

God's voice is not audible to me. Some people say they hear him speak. I've only heard him speak to me out loud once. Usually he speaks to me by moving in my spirit and giving me very clear impressions about what he wants to say to me. I'll write these thoughts down on my pad. Then I'll say, "Is this really you, Lord? Is this really what you are saying to me? Could this be the wanderings of my imagination or something greasy I ate for breakfast?" And God will patiently repeat his message to me again and again until I get it. That is why the paper and pen helps. I guess I may be a slow study, and it helps to go back and to see what God has been telling me.

Journaling is a big part of my communicating with God. Each day when I sit down with God, I open up my notebook (an inexpensive spiral bound student notebook) and record where I'm at as I start that day. It's my way to check in with God. Then I spend some time reading the Bible and when God gives me a new insight from His Word, I'll record those "ah-ha's" in my journal. Then I'll pray and as I talk with God if he gives me special messages or new insights, again these go down in the journal.

Sometimes I go back, several months or years, and read in my journal to see what I've come through or to get perspective on what God has done in my life. My journaling is free-form: some days I write a paragraph, some days nothing at all, and other days I'll write two pages. My wife has a journal from *Youth With A Mission* (YWAM – www.ywam.com). It has a set of Bible readings for each day and a space of five or six lines for each day to record your thoughts or what you are learning. She's used that method for 15 years and loves it. There are other ways to journal. A great resource on this topic is *Write for Your Soul: the How and Whys of Journaling*, by Jeff and Mindy Caliguire (www.soulcare.com).

OBSTACLES TO PRAYER

Finally, let me mention a few obstacles that might impede your prayer life. Prayer is such a powerful force for good in our lives. God can use it to change us for the better, to miraculously change our circumstances, and to pour all the spiritual blessings of the abundant life into our lives each day. You'd hate to miss any of that because there were spiritual obstacles hindering your prayer life.

The most common reason that people find God is not meeting them or meeting their needs is that they simply have not gotten around to asking Him. Many of us forget to pray, get too busy to pray, resort to praying "on the fly" as we dash from one thing to the next in our busy schedule. James 4:2 says, "You do not have, because you do not ask God."

I worry. I'm sure I'll eventually look back and discover I spent half my life worrying about things that never happened. Often I'm guilty of worrying about an issue, then seeking advice from my friends, perhaps reading various self-help books, or doing anything but praying regularly and consistently for that need. Now God knows what we need, and he wants to give it to us. And often he gives us what we need even when we don't bother to pray for it. But for some reason he chooses to unleash his power in special ways when we learn to ask him for his help. I think he just wants us to develop the habit of looking to him and asking for help. Then we need to expectantly open our arms so he can pour out the incredible riches and blessings he has for us.

Selfishness is another major issue that will block our prayer life. "When you ask, you do not receive because you ask with wrong motives, that you may spend what you get on your pleasures." (James 4:3) Ouch! Am I guilty of this! Always asking the Lord to help win the Publishers' Clearinghouse Sweepstakes and any other self- centered requests seem unavoidable. When I'm honest about my heart, what I really want is for God to make me prosperous, give me peace and leisure, and be sure I never face any more trials or pain or obstacles in my life. Sort of a "what's in it for me" theme often runs through my prayer life.

When I find that selfish attitude, I need to repent and ask God to give me His heart of mercy and compassion for the people in the world around me and to be grateful for all he's given me. When he breaks my heart and helps me see through his eyes, then I find my prayer requests focus more on Jesus and his mission, than my wants and desires. Proverbs 21:13 says, "If a man shuts his ear to the cry of the poor, he too will cry out and not be answered." God is committed to helping develop my character so that I reflect his love and compassion to the people who make up my world. When I get self-centered or become callus to the needs of others, it blocks my relationship with God.

Unconfessed sin is a different obstacle that can hinder your communication with God. Isaiah 59:2 says, "Your inadequacies have separated you from your God; your sins have hidden his face from you so he will not hear." Scripture refers to King David (who ruled Israel around 1000 BC) as "a man after God's own heart". David was chosen and blessed by God over many years. Yet at one point David fell into temptation at the sight of a beautiful young woman bathing on the roof of a house near his palace. He arranged to meet her, seduced her, and then got her pregnant. Rather than confessing and making right the wrong, David had her husband, a soldier fighting a war for Israel, sent to the front lines and then abandoned, so that he would sure to be killed. After the husband was dead, he married the woman.

David may have been a man after God's own heart, and he may have enjoyed a strong relationship with God for many years, but how do you think this affected his prayer life? David found the heavens were shut with an iron curtain. His fellowship with God was broken. After much personal suffering, God confronted David with his sin. David repented and was restored, but still paid a great price in negative consequences from that particular mistake.

God cares about our personal integrity. If we have unconfessed sin, if we have hurt another person, if we are cheating or stealing in some area of our lives, God will confront us and will press the issue with us. "What does the Lord require of you? To act justly and to love mercy and to walk humbly with your God." (Micah 6:8) If we fail to live this way, it will hinder our prayers until we make an about face and come back into line with God's way.

The final issue that can hinder your communication with God is to have a broken relationship in your life. This is so important. The Apostle John says, "Anyone who claims to be in the light, but hurts his brother is still in the darkness." (1John 2:9) "If anyone says, 'I love God', yet hates his brother, he is a liar. For anyone who does not love his brother, whom he has seen, cannot love God, whom he has not seen." (1John 4:20)

God is truly committed to building relationships of love between the people he's created. Other believers are God's primary resource to build healthy, positive relationships. In fact, God goes so far as to say that non-believers will be convicted and convinced about the truth and reality of God and his love in Jesus by what they see in the relational lives of believers. God cares about your relationship with your spouse, your children, your parents, your extended family, the folks at work, and those in the neighborhood. God cares about the people he has put in your world and wants to work through your life to reach those people. If you allow broken or damaged relationships to go on, you will ultimately hinder your own relationship with God. So if you reach a point where you are having trouble connecting with God, you might want to do a careful review of your relationships to see if they need some fence mending.

Before we close on this topic, I might also mention the role of obedience in maintaining open channels of communication with God. If God speaks to you when you pray and asks you to address some issue in your life, he really does expect you to obey. If you put it off, forget about it, rationalize it away, or neglect to act on it for any reason, it will close down your communication with God. Don't be like me! Sometimes I'm so stubborn, God has to hit me in my head with a piece of wood to get my attention. It's a painful way to grow. When God points out an issue, he wants you to work with him on it. If you ignore him, you can hardly expect him to spend a lot of time listening and responding to your prayer requests.

Learning to talk to God and hear him speak to us is such an incredibly important topic. I've barely scratched the surface here. There is so much more to learn, but God will teach it to you as you learn to talk to him. One other resource you might review on this subject is *Too Busy Not to Pray* by Bill Hybels. It's the best book I've read on prayer, and it will elaborate on more of the issues than we've touched on. It's full of practical help and motivation and it is well worth a read.

Discussion Questions – Chapter 7

1) What is your favorite form of communication and why?

2) Describe a time in your life when your communication broke down in a significant relationship. What happened as a result?

3) How do you go about finding times of solitude in your life? What do you use that time for? Could you carve out time alone to meet with God?

4) Think about some of the things you are most grateful for. Share some of these with the group. Then go home, make a list and share your gratitude with God.

5) Was there a part of the reading in this chapter that was particularly helpful for you, that made a connection in your mind, or that you disagree with? Share about that.

6) How could you use what you learned in this chapter to change your life in the coming week or months?

Chapter 8 – Learning from God

LIFE WITHOUT REGRETS

What shapes your goals in life? When you pause to examine your life, how do you evaluate where you are and where you are going? Lorraine Murry tells of her own success as a fast track executive in public relations. She made good money, had landed important promotions, and was given increased responsibility in her firm. But she found her success had a dark side. "As my responsibilities and pay increased so did the mental anguish. My job was like a 100-headed monster in a B-rated horror movie, always breathing down my neck and stalking me, even in the middle of the night. When I chopped the head off of one publication deadline, five more took its place."

"On Sunday morning, I began to dread Sunday evening, because it led to Monday morning. On Monday morning, I dreaded digging through the mounds of work awaiting me. Finally Murry found herself confronting a shocking question. "Was I making a living or was I making a dying? As I looked at my typical day with its frenzied commute, harried meetings, and endless deadlines, I realized suddenly what the answer was. My job had devoured my life."[9]

Do you want to live a life without regrets? When you get down the road a bit and you look back at what you've done with your life, how you've invested your time, attention, resources, and affections, do you want to have a sense of satisfaction for what you have done and who you have become? Most of us would say, "Yes! That's what I really want!" But my own experience in life is that many people, even the most and successful and admired people, look back on how they've lived their lives with profound regret. They wish they could do many things differently. But they can't. For most of us, once you realize you've squandered a significant opportunity in your life, it's in the past and it cannot be retrieved and done over. We don't get "mulligans" in real life.

God does not want you to live a life of regrets. He wants the very best for you and for me in both this life and in eternity. He's willing to commit his full resources to us to ensure we are able to invest our lives wisely and well so we finish the race of life with a real sense of satisfaction and fulfillment, rather that simply a heap of regrets and failures. As we begin to walk with Jesus and learn about our relationship with God, we will discover God wants to help reshape our perspectives, our understanding of the world. He wants to transform our attitudes, values, and priorities in life so we can begin to experience all of the spiritual and personal blessings he's designed us for as we walk through life.

We all begin life with a distorted set of values and perspectives. We may get a twisted worldview from our dysfunctional family of origin as I did, from our teenage friends or experiences, from our education, adult friends and family, the media, the Internet. I grew up in a very dysfunctional family. When I reached my early 30s, I was seeing a counselor for help with some family stress. He asked me about my childhood. I shared some of my experiences, and his shock was physically visible. He said, "I hate to tell you this, Bruce, but this type of behavior is not normal in a family. No, this is not normal." How was I supposed to know? I was well educated. I was a very successful corporate executive. But my family and childhood was the only one I'd ever known. I just assumed it was normal.

Scripture says, "There is a way that seems right to a man, but in the end it leads to death." (Proverbs 14:12) The world around us exerts tremendous influence in our lives by telling us and teaching us many things that simply are not true. If we are to learn to see and understand the world in our lives as they are, if we are going to benefit from all of the spiritual resources God wants to give us, if we are going to experience abundant life, we need to have our understanding reshaped by God himself. "The fear of the Lord is the foundation of life. Turning a man from the snares of death." (Proverbs 14:27)

THE TRANSFORMATIONAL POWER OF SCRIPTURE

I first met Jesus when I was living under the boardwalk in Ocean City, New Jersey. I've told the story in *Exploring God without Getting Religious*, but let me share one aspect of that experience. When my friend Moffit finally explained about how I could have a relationship with God through Jesus, it went like this. "It's like you look in the mirror at your life. If you like what you see—fine, you really don't need God. But if you don't like what you see, you can give your life to Jesus. He will keep the good in your life, throw out the bad, and replace it with his good."

That's really the best explanation I've ever heard for the process of transformation God wants to work in our lives. He's not out to destroy the good in us. Nor is he intent on making us into someone else. He wants to keep all of the good (after all, he designed it and created it when he made us—Psalm 139:13-16) and build on that foundation of good. He wants to take out the bad—the crooked, distorted, twisted elements of our personalities, and replace them with a new version of those parts of ourselves. The new version is reshaped to reflect his goodness, truth, and original design for us—so we can become all he created us to be.

The first year I walked with Jesus, all I had to guide me was my prayer relationship with God. I talked to him and listened to him. To be honest, my life was full of some pretty astounding sin and failure. After all, that's where I was when he found me. I really had no guidance to help me move my life closer to what Jesus wanted for me. The next summer I went back to Ocean City, and I met one of the people I had introduced to Jesus the previous year. She told me she met a guy who gave her a Bible and told her that they were God's love letters to his followers. She introduced me to this guy, and he gave me a paperback copy of the New Testament. Reading the Bible opened up a whole new chapter in my relationship with God. Learning from God's Word began the process of transforming my life into something much better than it had been.

Thornton Wilder's play, **Our Town**, tells the story of several people living in the fictional town of Grover's Corner, New Hampshire. The action takes place in the early 1900s, but the most interesting aspect of this play is the set. There isn't one. The entire play revolves around the relationships of the people. Wilder's point in eliminating the set is that he wants you to watch the people. He communicates a powerful message that the relationships are what the play is about and what life itself is about.

Each of us in our lives also has a role in a play. We live our lives on a set—our jobs, our home, our car, and our recreational activities—but what our lives are really about is relationships with people. The circumstances are just the set of the play. It is our relationships to people which produce the drama, passion, and action in our lives. That is why the Bible is so important. The Bible is a book about relationships. It is God's manual to help us learn how to guide and build our relationships so we can experience the abundant life he intends for each of us.

GOD'S WORD – A DAILY LIGHT

The Bible, God's Word, is full of helpful and practical advice to guide your life and increase your enjoyment of what God is doing in your life and in the world. It's full of historical information. If you want to learn about who Jesus is, what he said and what he did here on earth, it's in the Bible. It's full of knowledge about God. It will tell you who he is, what's important to him, how he's designed you to work, and how you can experience satisfaction and happiness. It will also tell you a lot about how he loves you and what he is doing in his relationship with you, both in this life and throughout eternity.

The Bible will give you guidelines for your life, clear ways to tell if you're heading in the right direction or if you need to make a course correction. You can check up on your attitudes and your relationships and find out how to get more joy from knowing yourself and from knowing others. It's all in the pages of the Bible. "[My friends] confronted me on the day of my disaster, but the Lord was my support." (Psalm 18:18) "You, Oh Lord, keep my lamp burning; my God turns my darkness into light." (Psalm 18:28) "I [Jesus] have come as a Light so no one who believes in me should stay in the darkness." (John 12:44) "All Scripture is God-breathed and is useful for teaching, rebuking, correcting, and training in righteousness, so that the person of God could be thoroughly equipped for every good work." (2 Tim 3:16-17)

Let me share just one passage of Scripture to illustrate how down-to-earth and practical the guidance is that appears in the Bible. The Apostle Paul is writing to the believers in Colossi and he says, "Put to death, therefore, whatever belongs to your earthly nature: sexual immorality, impurity, lust, evil desires, and greed, which are idolatry. Because of these the wrath of God is coming. You used to walk in these ways in the life you once lived. But now you must rid yourselves of such things as these: anger, rage, malice, slander, and filthy language from your lips. Do not lie to each other, since you have taken off your old self with its practices and have put on the new self, which is being renewed in knowledge in the image of its creator.

Here there is no Greek or Jew, circumcised or uncircumcised, barbarian or Scythian, slave or free. But Christ is all and is in all. Therefore, as God's chosen people, wholly and dearly loved, clothe yourself with compassion, kindness, humility, gentleness, and patience. Bear with each other and forgive whatever grievances you may have against one another. Forgive as the Lord forgives you and over all these virtues, put on love, which binds them all together, in perfect unity. Let the peace of Christ rule in your hearts, since as members of one body you are called to peace, and be thankful. Let the word of Christ dwell in you richly as you teach and admonish one another with all wisdom, and as you sign psalms, hymns and spiritual songs with gratitude in your heart to God. And whatever you do, whether in word or deed, do it all in the name of the Lord Jesus giving thanks to God the Father through Him." (Col 3:5-17)

Here is one passage of twelve verses from one chapter of one of the 64 books of the Bible. I could study just these twelve verses and apply them to my life for as long as I live, and I would still have issues to work on and grow in each day. You will find God's Word is incredibly rich, practical and helpful in your every day life. No matter how long you read it and study it, you will always find God giving you abundant insights, which will encourage your walk with him and your love of life and other people. I've been studying the Bible for over thirty years, I earned a Bachelors' degree in Biblical Studies, and did Masters' level work at seminary, and yet God's Word is still fresh, relevant, and practical in my life everyday.

BIBLE TRANSLATIONS

In order to learn from the Bible, you'll need to understand what it is saying. That is why the translation of the Bible you read is important. At last count there were 247 English translations of the Bible. This overabundance of versions often confuses the new believer. Trust me – it confuses mature believers as well. Some translations, like the King James, are traditional and revered by many. Of course, that particular translation was written in 1611 as a contemporary alternative to the Latin text and may be hard for today's reader to understand. More modern versions include the Good News (TEV), New International (NIV), and The Message, a paraphrase.

Let me demonstrate the difference the translation can make in your ability to understand and apply a passage from God's Word. Here's a small section from the book of Titus (Titus 3:5-6), which talks about how God saved us through Jesus Christ. In the *King James Version* it reads: "Not by works of righteousness, which we have done, but according to his mercy he saved us, by the work of regeneration and renewing of the Holy Ghost; which he shed on us abundantly through Christ Jesus our Savior."

In the *Good News Bible* (Today's English Version): "He [God] saved us. It was not because of any good deeds that we ourselves have done, but because of his own mercy that he saved us through the Holy Spirit, who gives us new birth and new life by washing us. God poured out the Holy Spirit abundantly on us through Jesus Christ our Savior."

In the *New International Version*: "He [God] saved us, not because of the righteous things we have done, but because of his mercy. He saved us through the washing of rebirth and renewal by the Holy Spirit, whom he poured out on us generously through Jesus Christ Our Savior."

And in *The Message*: "He [God] saved us from all that. It was all his doing; we had nothing to do with it. He gave us a good bath and we came out of it new people, washed inside and out by the Holy Spirit. Our Savior Jesus poured out new life so generously."

Avoid Bibles with a lot of commentary from some other author, such as the Thompson Chain Reference Bible. To learn from God, you need to read His Word and ask the Holy Spirit to teach you what it means for your life. Don't spend your time listening to what a lot of "experts" say a particular passage means. The most important place to invest your time is alone with God and his Word or with fellow believers who are all struggling to learn from God and apply his principles to our daily life, here in the beginning of the 21st century. After you have a lot more maturity in the Lord, and you've studied the Word and learn to hear God's voice speaking to you in your need, some of these reference tools or study aids may prove helpful. But at the beginning, they may simply distract you from hearing God's voice through Scripture.

READING AND STUDY STRATEGIES

God wrote the Bible so it could be understood by ordinary, every day people. He used real human beings to actually write the books of the Bible. They are set in the historical context of the real world time in which they were written. God breathed his thoughts and wisdom through these human writers with the Holy Spirit's guidance in a miraculous way. The result is a book that is timely and relevant and speaks right to the issues of our hearts, just as it has done to people of various times and cultures for the 3,500 years it's been read. Even today, in our modern world, the Bible is still the top-selling book in the world, the most read, and the most used volume across people groups and cultures all around the globe.

You don't need to be an expert to read and understand the Bible. Remember, they are love letters from a heavenly Father who loves His children. He wants to provide guidance, encouragement, and support through this book. It's not about how much you know, it's about how you let get God's love and His Word penetrate your heart and change your life. "We know that all possess knowledge. Knowledge puffs up, but love builds up. The man who thinks he knows something does not yet know, as he ought to know. But the man who loves God is known by God." (1Cor 8:1-3)

When I study a Bible passage, I ask myself three questions:
1. What does it say?
2. What does it mean?
3. How does it apply to my life?

These are also the study questions I recommend you use for a small group (2-12 people) who sit down and study the Bible together. It gets at the heart of the passage and how God wants to apply it in a practical way to our lives today. That's what he wants to do each time you read His Word. He wants to speak to your heart and help you become a better person and enjoy the abundant life Jesus offers.

Some people write notes in the pages of the Bible when they study and learn different things. Others I know use a student highlighter or use different colors to mark key passages or phrases or words that stand out when they read. I don't do either. I prefer to leave the page unmarked in the expectation that each time I read a passage I will learn something fresh, something new, something different from God—usually I do. You should do whatever helps you learn and retain what the Bible has to say. Several topical indexes of helpful Bible passages are included in the Appendix of this book.

You might want to experiment to find a Bible reading or study habit that works best for you. My wife often reads the Bible through sequentially, from Genesis, the first book, to Revelation, the last book. For many years, she read the whole Bible in one year using this strategy. I like to read continuously, but I read a page or two from the Old Testament, a page or two from Psalms and Proverbs (two devotional books in the middle of the Bible), and a page or two from the New Testament. I read each part of the Bible in order, but I want to get a variety of God's counsel from His Word. There are books that help you read through the whole Bible, which could be helpful in learning how to learn from God's Word (see Walk through the Bible Ministry – www.walkthru.org).

When I was younger, I started with a book and read and studied a chapter each morning until I was finished with that book. There are lots of Bible study guides you can check out if you get stuck. But the most important thing is to find an approach that connects you to the heart of God each day so that he can speak to you of His love for you and so he can guide you into new growth in your life.

Let me leave you with one warning about the Bible before we close this topic. Don't fall into the trap of worshipping the Bible. There are some believers who have elevated the Bible to a position far above Jesus and God the Father himself. When you attend a church that has fallen into this trap, you can easily get confused because they actually worship the Bible: Bibliolatry is the term for idolizing the Bible in place of God. The Bible is simply one of the means God gives us to come into a healthy relationship with him. The principle means is Jesus, who is God himself. That's who we worship. The Holy Spirit is given that Christ may live in us, our hope for today and for eternity. The Holy Spirit is also a person of God and is there to comfort, encourage, and instruct us that we might become more like Jesus. God the Father is also worthy of our "worth ship" where we praise him for who he is and how he loves.

The Bible is God's baby talk. In order to communicate with us, his knowledge and character being so much higher than our finite abilities—he speaks in baby talk in the Bible. Nicky Gumbal, the founder of the Alpha Course, says that idolizing the Bible is a bit like a fellow who went out and bought a new car. He brought it home, parked it, took the owner's manual inside and began to scrutinize it. He learned the book inside and out, finally was able to quote long passages from memory, and then went to language school so he could read his manual in the original Japanese. Yet in all of this, he missed the point - the manual was to help him get the best possible experience out of driving his car, which sat moldering at the curb. Gumbal's analogy is quite right. The Bible is designed to help us get the most out of our relationship with God. It is not an end in itself.

OTHER WAYS TO LEARN FROM GOD

The most important way to learn from God is to meet with him alone and to read His word and let him teach you from the Bible and through the still, small voice of the Holy Spirit speaking to you. There are a number of other ways to learn that may be useful and build on what you are learning one-on-one with God. Studying the Bible with a group of people can be most instructive. What God is teaching someone else—through the Bible and their life experience—may prove enlightening to you as well.

A Bible study group could be as few as two people or as many as 12 people. Once a group gets over 12, the group dynamics cause some to stop sharing and others to share too much. So I suggest you keep group at 12 or less if you really hope to have everyone participate and benefit. If more want to join, simply split into two groups so the size stays in the appropriate range. When you study as a group, begin in prayer just as you would on your own. Ask God to guide you and to speak to each person through His Word. He will. Then read the passage. It helps to do it out loud. Ask the three basic questions: what does it say, what does it mean, and how does it apply to my life? We'll talk more about small groups and community in the next chapter, but a couple of pointers on group dynamics for Bible study may be useful here.

Sometimes you want to study with a group of believers. These may be people at about the same stage of faith as you are, or a mixed group with some older, more mature believers, and some younger in the Lord. It's also a great learning experience to study the Bible in a group composed of some believers and some seekers. The believers get a chance to share their faith and experience with those who are still investigating God (as we describe in Chapter 11). The seekers really focus the group discussion on key issues where God can make a dramatic difference in people's lives. All will be encouraged by reconnecting with the basics of the faith.

Finally, you might choose to start a Bible study group with a group composed entirely of seekers or even people that are not sure there is a God. The dynamic will be different, but God will also act in life changing ways in this environment. To see your friends have their spiritual lights turned on as they study God's word and meet Jesus is a life changing experience you will never forget. Check out Garry Poole's book, *Seeker Small Groups* to learn more about effective Bible studies with seekers.

Christian books can be a great source of encouragement and can help you learn more from God. I often read through a book on some issue of faith in addition to reading the Bible in my times alone with the Lord. At times I will vary my Bible reading by taking some time off to read a book on a special topic. You want to look for books that will encourage your love for Jesus and help you grow closer to the Father. I've mentioned several books in the course of this text that are worth reading. Others I've read which have been helpful include:

- *Mere Christianity* by C.S. Lewis
- *The Case for Christ* by Lee Stroble
- *Christianity for Skeptics*, by Steve Kumar
- *Christianity is Jewish* by Eve Shaefer
- *Passion & Purity* and *Shadow of the Almighty*, by Elizabeth Elliott
- *His Needs, Her Needs* (great book on marriage) by Williard F. Harley, Jr.
- *Traveling Light* by Max Lucado
- *Wild at Heart* (a book for men) by John Eldridge
- *Questions of Life* by Nicki Gumbal

These are just a few of my favorites. In the Appendix you will find a list of a number of different types of books that may appeal to you and may be helpful to the growth of your spiritual life. Not every book will be a good fit for you. Each of us likes different styles of writing and different approaches to various topics. You may have to try a few until you find what works for you. Just keep looking for those things that draw you closer to God and that stimulate your love for Jesus and other people.

TEST THE SPIRITS

A note of caution! Not every book written by or for Christians is a good book to read. You will have to exercise some judgment and discernment about what you read. Scripture teaches that there are false prophets - wolves in sheep's clothing according to God - sneaking among the flock looking for victims. (Acts 20:29-31) We are also told, "Do not believe every spirit, but test the spirits to see whether they are from God." (1John 4:1-3)

I recently came across a book entitled, *Hating for Jesus*. The author's message was that unless you hated yourself, your family, your friends, your work, and even nature itself—unless you hated everything God has put in this world— you couldn't really say you love Jesus. So to love Jesus you have to hate everybody and everything else including yourself. This is so completely the opposite of everything we see revealed in Scripture about Jesus and about God's love and grace. Jesus said, "No, it's a lot simpler than you think. Unless you love like the little children who come to sit on my knee, you won't get the accurate picture of the spiritual life."

Thank goodness this particular distortion of a book has gone out of print, but it does illustrate the point that it is important to test the spirits and see if what you are reading squares up with the rest of what you know about God through Scripture and experience.

In addition to books there are seminars, tapes, and sometimes radio and television programs that can help your faith to grow. Family Life's *"Weekend to Remember"* is a great seminar for married couples. I've gone on it, and it is a real eye-opener. I learned a lot about all the good gifts God has given me in my marriage and my spouse that I didn't know after 20 years of married life. I recommend it. Willow Creek Community Church has a great resource center (www.seeds.willowcreek.org/wc/) which offers books, CDs, and DVDs of solid Christian teaching. Sermons or church services are another way to learn more about God and to learn more from God. You can order sermons on CD from Pastor Bill Hybels and others at Willow Creek Community Church or download them as an MP3 file.

Many local congregations have active fellowships for believers and good teaching and sermons in their Sunday programs. But this is the area that you will most need discernment to sort out the good from the bad. You simply cannot assume because the organization bills itself as a Christian church, they will be teaching about God, Jesus, or the Bible. Some offer quite a lot of help in following Jesus. Many are somewhat of a mixed bag—some stuff driven by a genuine love relationship with God and much else that is driven by all kinds of human agendas. Some, I'm sorry to say, are absolutely horrific or actually anti-Christian in their behavior or beliefs.

Many will remember the church started by Jim Jones in Los Angeles in the 1980's. Eventually his teaching led his congregation so far astray from God and his principles that they all moved to Guyana and eventually took part in a mass suicide of 900 adults and children under the charismatic leadership of Rev. Jones. From time to time, what appear to be healthy churches veer off into heresy or control and domination by leaders so they become a cult that is try to overpower and rule the lives of their members. The Boston Church of Christ, now the International Church of Christ, is a current day example of a group that began as a Christian ministry, which has been accused of cult-like practices. See www.reveal.org to learn more about this type of church dysfunction.

Test the spirits! Read 1John 4 and learn how to spot false prophets from God's Word. Test what a church tells you against your own experience of God's love and grace, against your knowledge of God's word, and with the wisdom of other mature believers you respect. James 1:5 says, "If any of you lacks wisdom, you should ask God, who gives generously to all without finding fault, and it will be given to him." So proceed with caution, stay close to the Lord, and ask God for spiritual wisdom and discernment—which he promises to give freely and generously.

Discussion Questions – Chapter 8

1) Think about your childhood and teen years – did you ever regret decisions you made or failed to make? Give an example and describe how it made you feel.

2) Have you ever thought about what you will think or feel when you evaluate your life at the end? What will enable you to look back on a life without regrets?

3) What role does the Bible have in stimulating your relationship with God?

4) What is one relationship lesson you have learned from the Bible that really works or that has helped you in your life?

5) If you spent half as much time with God as you now spend on Facebook, e-mail, Twitter, or texts…how much would your relational time for God increase?

6) Describe one area of your life you'd like to see God change. How might you use what you learned in this chapter to change that area of your life in the coming week or months?

Chapter 9 - Building Community

THE RELATIONAL DISCIPLINES

The three spiritual disciplines we've discussed in the last three chapters (the personal disciplines) may not have been a complete surprise to you. If you have had any exposure to spiritual things, you have some notion of the value of seeking God, praying, and learning about him. Now lest you run off and decide to join a monastery or retreat to a mountaintop cave where you can better develop these habits, let me stop you right here. These personal spiritual disciplines are not enough. You really can't become the person God has designed you to be if all you have are these three disciplines. God has designed us as people who need people. In order to grow to become more like Jesus, to experience the "abundant life" God promises to give us, we also need to develop the three relational disciplines.

The first of these, the need for community, is perhaps one of the hardest for Americans to develop. As Americans, we so love our independence. We want to be self-sufficient, competent, self-supporting, in charge, calling the shots. Yet it's clear that everything about following Jesus requires developing certain relational skills. The short letter of 1 John does a masterful job of explaining this principle. "If anyone says, "I love God," yet hates his brother, he is a liar. For anyone who does not love his brother, whom he has seen, cannot love God, whom he has not seen. And he has given us this command: Whoever loves God must also love his brother." (1 John 4:20-21)

There are 285 imperatives, or commands, given to followers of Jesus in the New Testament. Every one of them concerns some aspect of how we are to relate to fellow believers or to those who don't yet know Jesus. "Love one another, forgive each other, make allowances for differences, bear one another's

85

burdens, pray for each other, counsel one another, be patient, kind, rejoice in the truth, don't keep account of wrongs." These and many other instructions teach us how to relate to fellow believers, to those who don't yet know Jesus, to those who persecute us, and to worldly authorities.

It becomes obvious that it is impossible to live out the qualities of life that define a follower of Jesus unless we are in relationships where we can learn to do this for one another. We need to be in community, in the context of a small group of friends who know us and love us, if we are to apply the things we learn in the Christian life in any meaningful way. All too often we see believers who are trying to live a spiritual life on their own. This is one of the consequences of the excessive focus on individualism in our society. It simply cannot work. It cuts across the grain of how God has designed us as human beings. We need relationships with each other to survive as well as to thrive.

FALLING FROM GRACE

Even among well-known Christian leaders, it is quite common to find those with a robust devotional life, who have no relational community. In most cases, when you see a prominent person of faith fall from grace into moral or ethical failure, it almost always comes from a failure to live in the context of community. Most of these people have an excellent knowledge of God's Word; they pray often and are very involved in Christian activities. Yet they fall prey to some moral temptation that destroys their integrity and their ministry. Why? No community!

Not too long ago, one of the largest and most prominent churches in an Eastern state was shocked by the moral failure of their senior pastor. The church was large, apparently healthy, and growing. They had entered into a $4 million expansion campaign to handle the multiplying crowds of happy, excited believers. One Sunday morning, the pastoral leader of this congregation got up and confessed he had been unfaithful to his wife. In fact, he had been having adulterous relationships with four different women in his church simultaneously. After his confession, he resigned. Simply reading the newspapers provides a steady stream of other sad illustrations of what can happen to even the best of Christian leaders when they live without accountable friendships.

Let's be honest. It is all too easy for any of us to deceive ourselves. Left on our own, we see ourselves as the person we want to be, hope to be, or wish we were. As Scripture tells us, "Surely the mind and heart of man are deceptive." (Psalm 64:6) I learned one of the most profound truths about human nature in college when I read this insight ascribed to Soren Kierkegaard: "Man alone is sincere. At the entrance of a second person, hypocrisy begins." Human nature seems to cause even the most honest of us into a pattern of spin doctoring where we try to put the best face on what is often a rather uneven performance as the person we aspire to be. We all need the dose of reality only trusted friends can provide so we can grow to be more and more like Jesus. We all need community so God can help us to become the kind of person we were created to be.

A BIBLICAL VIEW OF COMMUNITY

God himself demonstrates the importance of community. As the Creator of all that is, God could have designed the system anyway he wanted to. Yet he voluntarily designed things so he could live in community. The Trinity, the persons of the Father, Son and Holy Spirit, demonstrate that in the essential foundation of the Godhead himself, our creator is committed to community. These three persons of God have existed together since the dawn of creation. We learn that Jesus was present at the beginning, in fact, "through him all things were made." (John 1:3) In the account of creation in the Book of Genesis, the Holy Spirit is described as having an instrumental role in the process. (Genesis 1:2) From the very beginning of time, and throughout history, God has chosen to live and work and fellowship in the community of the three persons of the Trinity.

Scripture makes it clear that each member of this "Community of God" has a separate and distinct role to play. The Father appears to handle the authority and justice attributes of God. Jesus is God Incarnate – all the aspects of God expressed in a human form. Jesus is our friend, our Savior, and the head of the people of God – the church. Finally, the Holy Spirit is given to each believer when we accept Jesus and follow him. The Spirit's job is to teach us, to comfort us, and to protect us until we are rejoined with Jesus. (John 14:25-27)

God has designed each one of us and together all the people of God in this same dependent, interactive way. When you read 1Corinthians 12: 12-27, the clearest description of the life of believers together, we learn several important principles. Every believer has been given a unique set of spiritual gifts, personality and motivation. God has designed every one of us to do one thing better than anyone else in the world. This passage teaches us that we all have unique roles to play. As the people of God, we should expect each believer to look and act differently, much like the different parts of our physical body.

Yet we all are joined together by the one Spirit, and we all serve under the leadership of Christ Jesus. Everyone is needed. No one is more or less important than anyone else. Just like the three persons of the Trinity, each one of us has been created for community. Until we find our proper place in the Body of Christ, we cannot discover the highest purpose for which we were made.

Jesus demonstrates the need for community in his life here on earth. While living as one of us in the historical context of 1st century Israel, Jesus was both "fully God and fully man." He shared all of the attributes of a human being while not having his personhood as God limited. We see glimpses of this when he walks on the water, heals the blind, and raises the dead. Jesus is all of God poured into a human form. He told his disciples, "If you have seen me you have seen the Father." Yet Jesus chose to live in community. He had a group of about 120 followers. Of those, he selected 12 people to focus on building into an accountable small group, or what we would call a community. When you read the Gospels, the story of Jesus life here on earth, his friendship with these 12 individuals is woven throughout the text. There is simply no way to understand who Jesus is or why he came to earth without viewing it through the lens of his community, his band of friends.

Jesus passed this requirement for community onto each of us who follow him to this day. "I have set you an example that you should do as I have done for you...no servant is greater than his master." (John 13:12-17) Later in the same address he tells us how he wants us to imitate his life of relational community: "A new command I give to you. Love one another. As I have loved you, so you must love one another. By this will all men know that you are my disciples, if you love one another." (John 13:34, 35)

The Apostle Paul did more for the spread of the Christian faith than anyone else in his century. His pastoral letters, and the theological explanations contained therein, not only shaped the faith of those in the early church, they have gone on to shape much of our own thinking and practice as Christ followers in the 21st century. Just like Jesus, Paul lived out his faith journey in the context of community. When he went on his first missionary journey to Crete and Asia Minor, he went with Barnabus and John Mark. Read the Book of Acts and the Letters of Paul in the New Testament. Every time you encounter Paul, he has a band of friends who are helping him in his ministry and supporting him in his personal life. In spite of the fact that he lived the nomadic existence of an itinerant evangelist and church planter, he almost always managed to bring community with him even when he was in prison. Paul's life vividly underscores the importance of and the power of community for the Christ follower.

COMMUNITY IS UNNATURAL

It should be clear by now that community is required to grow to health and maturity in the Christian life. Jesus commands us to love one another as the most powerful testimony we can give to the truth and reality of God. Furthermore, we have powerful examples throughout Scripture to convince us of the necessity of community for the life of faith. Having said that, in all honesty, I must confess I find the whole notion of community somewhat unnatural.

My observations of the humans who inhabit my world indicate that rather than seeking out the fellowship of community, our natural bent is towards isolation and individualism. I don't know if this is simply a problem of the American experience or a 21st century issue. When I read the Psalms, I see over and over the authors' deep feelings of loneliness, affliction, and despair. There is a reaching out to God, but still a sense that one is between a rock and a hard place and truly alone. Among my contemporaries, I would say most of the men I know would have trouble identifying one friend in their life let alone a small band of peers who know and support them. Women seem to be more relational and make friends easier, but again, the most common circumstance is for women to feel pretty isolated outside of their immediate family and work context.

Why this tilt towards isolation rather than community? One big reason is the sin problem. We all have one. Even after we have trusted Jesus, and our sins have been forgiven (and they have – including past, present and future sins), we struggle with the battle between the habits of our "old nature" and the "new person" we are becoming in Christ Jesus. In Romans 7:15-25 the Apostle Paul describes his struggle with sin and his old nature. "For what I do is not the good I want to do; no, the evil I do not want to do – this I keep on doing." All of us in Christ though redeemed and on the road to becoming more like Jesus, wrestle with this same spiritual issue articulated by Paul.

Our instinct when we are hurt or wounded is to want to hide. When my mother died this summer, I found myself depressed, moody, and withdrawn. I didn't want to be with people and when I was, I had nothing to say. This was not the result of sin or a battle with my old nature; it was simply my response to difficult circumstances. They say the two most common reactions to stress are "fight or flight." Like most men, when under pressure, I head for the cave. I just want to be alone so I can lick my wounds and feel sorry for myself.

My good friend Karl told me that when his mother died, he withdrew from relationships at home and at work. He tried to be alone as much as possible. He even changed cars on the commuter train into Chicago because he simply did not want to have to relate to people he had seen for years. He shared, "I knew my Mom was with Jesus, and I knew I should not be depressed, but I still was." That was exactly the experience I went through.

Now I've been told that when stressed, women run to community, and men head for isolation. But I'm not sure that's always the case. When my friend Margie lost her Dad a few years ago, she would sink out of sight for weeks at a time as she worked through the grieving process. In her case her best friends were in her immediate family and her extended family. They were all wallowing through the deep waters of grief and loss themselves. She really didn't have a community of believing friends to turn to, so she withdrew into isolation.

In fact, the more we need help from others, for some perverse reason, the more likely we are to avoid others or put on a false front to deceive others about our need. "Fake it 'till you make it" becomes our only strategy for coping with our pain and our need. Men in particular, have a high need to have others think of them as competent. (Yes, ladies, that is why they always refuse to stop the car and ask for directions!) If you are driving in the car, probably the worse this trait will produce is that you get lost and are late for dinner. Yet in other circumstances the outcome can be tragic.

Not too long ago, I got a letter from a guy who shared about his friend Stan. "Unknown to all of us, Stan was diagnosed as bipolar seven years ago and has been struggling all along. He seemed to be a well-adjusted husband and father of three nice kids. Then he ran into a series of unfortunate circumstances (multiple job layoffs in the same year) due to no fault of his own, but he took it very hard. He never showed it externally however, and was typically very jovial and upbeat in public. None of his friends even knew there was a problem until we got the call that he was dead. Stan committed suicide by throwing himself out of his sixth floor office window."

COMMUNITY IS UNAMERICAN

Not only is community unnatural, it seems pretty un-American as well. Our American culture has long evidenced strong traits that drive people to be loners, independent, isolated and self-sufficient. The history of our nation's development rode on the "pioneer spirit" constantly pushing westward, looking for new opportunities. It may be that our country has attracted more than its share of restless, proactive, Attention Deficit Disorder type personalities from all the countries that have added to our melting pot. These were not the people who were content with the status quo. They were willing to strike out on their own to remake their destiny. Loners shaped our country – Daniel Boone, Davy Crockett, Kit Carson and Jim Bridger exemplify the kind of heroes that dominate the pages of our history books.

The Marlboro Man, one of the classic icons of American advertising, captures the spirit of these historical models and presents it in a fresh, modern version. First created by the Leo Burnett Agency in 1957, this ad image is still one of the most powerful and enduring brand symbols fifty years later. He is alone, in control, riding his horse where no man has dared go before. John Wayne reflects this same idealized American man in many of the movie roles he played. "The Quiet Man," "Rooster Cogburn," and "Sargent Striker" all capture this portrait of the American man: a guy of very few words who rarely shows his feelings, strong, tough, and almost always…alone. Clint Eastwood continued the same themes, and the role model of the strong but isolated man in his famous cowboy roles and as the police detective Dirty Harry. Jason Bourne of the *Bourne Identity* is another example of the same.

COMMUNITY IS CRITICAL

While it may be true that human nature and American culture may steer us away from community, it is absolutely essential to have some community if we are to grow in our walk with Jesus. We all have a built in tendency to become self absorbed to the point of addiction. The reason consumerism and materialism are rampant in American society is that our material wealth as a country allows us to consume almost without limits. Our theme song becomes, "What's in it for me?"

Unfortunately, this is true even after we meet Jesus and begin to walk with him. Listen to how one young believer, Donald Miller, described this phenomenon in his own life. "The most difficult lie I have ever contended with is this: 'Life is a story about me.' No drug is as powerful as the drug of self. No rut in the road is so deep as the one that says I am the world, the world belongs to me, and all people are characters in my play. There is no addiction so powerful as self-addiction." [10]

Miller, the author of *Blue like Jazz*, puts his finger on the heart of the issue. This is what our sin problem is really all about. Each of us, in our own way wants to play God. The entire human race and each of us individually have this habit of rewriting the script so we get what we want from life. I am often guilty of wanting to make the world revolve around me and my needs and desires. I expect God to be my cosmic butler and fetch whatever I want when I want it. Left on my own, I find I am constantly trying to manipulate my circumstances and those around me to create a certain image of myself, a certain experience for myself, or a particular outcome that will bring the fulfillment I seek. Me, me, me – it's all about me!

God desires community for each one of us because it is the most effective way to set us free from self-addiction. Community is also God's most powerful tool for us to discover our unique gifts and talents as well as God's special purpose for each of us in life. Our small band of friends is a principle influence the Lord uses to help us become more and more like Jesus. Finally, believing community is the most powerful witness we can offer the world to demonstrate the reality and love of God.

The rub about relationships (hence, community, where we are really known), is our fear that if someone gets to know us, the real person that we keep hidden from others, they might not love us. They might instead reject us. Donald Miller points out, "To be in a relationship with God is to be loved purely and furiously. And a person who thinks himself unlovable cannot be in a relationship with God because he can't accept who God is; a being that is love. We learn we are lovable from other people. That is why God tells us so many times to love each other."[11]

When a believer relies on the personal disciplines alone, it is easy to get off track and end up thinking faith is a matter of assenting to some propositions about God. Far too many people fall into the error of thinking that faith is about conceptual knowledge: simply a matter of being able to say, "Yes, I believe this doctrine, or this theological statement to be true." Others mistakenly conclude faith is something I do – sort of a spiritual activities checklist I run through periodically. "Yup, I went to church this week, I read my Bible, I helped an old lady across the street, I didn't cuss, and I did not watch any bad movies."

God's primary concern is not our dedication to a set of cognitive beliefs, nor is our faith primarily about what we do. Rule keeping won't get us any points, nor will accomplishing great things for the Kingdom of God. We are saved by faith, by God's grace and not by any attempts at righteousness on our own (Galatians 2:16).

God's primary concern is what kind of people we are and what kind of people we are becoming. God looks at the heart. Of course, we can observe something of what is going on in our own heart, by examining our behavior towards others and by our speech. As Jesus pointed out, just as a good tree produces good fruit, we can get some read on the heart by the externals. Yet God's focus is to help us become more like Jesus. As a person, I'm still going to have the unique characteristics that make me Bruce Dreisbach, but I will exude more and more of the sweet fragrance of Christ from my life. Community is God's principle growth environment to help this life transformation take place for you and for me.

HOW TO CREATE COMMUNITY

How can you find community? Given what I've told you – it's an unnatural and un-American activity – don't expect it to be easy. This may be the hardest spiritual discipline to develop. But it is also the one discipline that pays the richest rewards. I was having dinner with a couple the other night. Larry mentioned he and Joyce have been in a small group for over 35 years. Early in their marriage, when they had several pre-school kids, they realized how many marriages in their neighborhood were on the rocks and breaking up. In an instinctive reaction towards self-defense, they called up two other couples and started a small group.

Since its beginning in 1970, this community has grown and ministered to both spiritual and practical needs of the participants and their families. Sick children, lost jobs, marital conflict, baby showers, weddings and funerals – through all the high and low points of life this group has prayed, encouraged and loved each other through life. Their nickname for the group is "The Family." That's exactly how this diverse group of believers functions, as an extended family of God. To be known, to be loved, to know and love others – this is the payback from community.

Let's talk for a moment about specific steps you can take to find community for yourself. The key ingredient for success in this endeavor is prayer. God knows you; he knows your heart and what sort of friends you need. He is committed to helping you develop community. He also knows the heart of people who may be in your life who could be a good friend. Simply ask God to help you reach out, find the right people, and give you divine opportunities to be a friend to others. Trust him and keep praying as you work through the rest of the steps.

INITIATE IN THE MARGINS

One of the major steps to finding friends is to accept the responsibility to initiate. If you want real friends, if you want community, you will have to initiate. Most of us are sitting around waiting for someone to notice us, say hello, introduce themselves, ask a question about us, and invite us to something…Well, guess what? If everybody waits for someone else to initiate, nothing is going to happen!

During my corporate business career, I used to have to attend these awful business mixers where everybody stood around with a drink in hand and felt awkward and uncomfortable. It was like what I imagine dying a terrifyingly slow and painful death would be like. Then I realized everybody in the room felt exactly like I did. They just didn't know what to do about it. Recognizing there is one subject everyone likes to talk about (that would be "me") I came up with a half dozen questions that would help people start to talk. "So how are you connected to this organization (sponsor of the mixer)?" "Tell me about your family?" "What do you like to do for fun?" I jotted these on an index card, shoved it in my shirt pocket and wandered around the room chatting amiably with everyone. Or at least it induced them to chat freely with me. Just like that, I went from wallflower to gregarious extrovert. If anything is going to happen in your relationships, you will have to initiate.

Before you head off to work your networks, let me make another observation. You make friends in the margins of your life. If you don't have any margin, any free or unscheduled time in your life, you won't have many friends. Richard Swenson's book, *Margins*, says most of us have overloaded our lives, and consequently, they are full of hurry, anxiety, fatigue, and red ink. When was the last time you took a walk in the park, sat on a bench, watched the squirrels and clouds and just reflected? If you don't have the friends you want or the kind of friendships you want (even with your spouse) it may be from a lack of margins. You simply have not made enough time available to have the kinds of relationships that feed you as a person, that become community. Too busy is a choice and it can have extremely negative outcomes for your relationships and priorities in life.

YOUR RELATIONAL NETWORK

As you pray through the people God has put in your life, who might have the potential to become your community, it helps to do an inventory of who we know. Take a blank sheet of paper. List the names of people you see frequently: daily or several times per week. These could be family, neighbors, or colleagues at work. Then list those you see occasionally: two or three times per month. Finally, list those you see infrequently, less than once a month, but whom you would like to get to know better.

This list begins to form an outline we can pray over as we ask God to help us develop friends and community. As you pray, think about the personal characteristics of each of these people. There are three characteristics that you should look for in a potential friend. The first quality we hope for is **teachability**. Are they open to us, willing to learn and receive from us, or do they always insist on their own way? I have a friend who is the retired CEO of a major defense contractor. Although he is a very successful man, I see him learning from everyone. He learns from his grandchildren, from his gardener, even from the waiter in a restaurant. He defines "teachability" for me. I have other friends who are in their early twenties, barely out of college. Yet you can't teach them a thing. They are absolutely sure they know everything and are 100% correct on any opinion they express. Don't waste your relational time on people like this.

The next quality you want to look for is **availability**. We are all too busy. But is this potential friend willing to make time for you? If they are too busy to make time to be with you or always have to cancel because "something else came up," they don't really want to invest their scarce time in your friendship. I was trying to get to know a young engineer I met at church. We agreed to meet at my house for coffee once a week at 6am in the morning. He had to leave at 7am sharp to get to his job in a nearby city on time. A bout three weeks out of four, Skip would turn up at 6:45, have a quick belt of coffee between mumbled apologies and then he would bolt after 15 minutes. Week after week I sat there waiting for Skip and felt frustrated. At the end of the day, I simply had to accept that Skip was not that interested in building a friendship.

The last characteristic that shows someone has the potential to become a good friend is **mutual affinity**. Do you find the person interesting? Do you have things you share in common? These could be hobbies, or an interest in discussing big ideas, or a love of fixing mechanical things in the garage. Often people who share a similar age and stage in life can become great friends. Alternatively, sometimes someone much older or younger can become a good friend. Scripture encourages older men and older women to mentor younger men and women. When we lived in the suburbs of Chicago, we became good friends with a couple who were probably 20 years our seniors. We had pre-schoolers but their children were grown and gone from home. Libby and Glen loved us, modeled a healthy marriage, gave us great parenting advice and became a surrogate family when our own families were far away. Their friendship had a major impact on our long-term success as a couple and as parents.

IT'S A PROCESS

Finding friends, building community, is a lot like mining for gold. When you mine for gold, you have to process a lot of dirt. In fact, most of the technical advances in gold mining over the past century involve finding better ways to process more dirt more efficiently. Yet the successful miner never loses sight of the fact that the objective is not processing dirt, but rather it's finding gold nuggets. It's the gold nuggets that pay for the whole enterprise. Likewise, in finding friends and building community. You may have to sort through a lot of people and many entry level relationships to find a handful of good friends.

When we moved to New Hampshire, we started this process from scratch. We regularly invited people over to dinner to try to get to know them and possibly initiate a relationship. My wife, Martie often compares the process of building a friendship to playing tennis. I hit the ball over the net to you, and then you hit it back to me. If we each keep that up, we are playing tennis. If one of us lets the ball drop and doesn't send it back…no game. At one point Martie estimated that we had invited about 150 individuals, couples, or families over for dinner. How many would you suppose invited us back? Not many. More often than not, we would initiate in a relationship, and the ball was never returned. Perhaps after a few sputtering volleys, the game just dies out. My guess is that only 10 or 15 of those we invited actually became good friends. What wonderful friends they are! We have tasted and shared life together, we have prayed for and encouraged each other; we have cried tears of grief over tragedies and loss. We had to process a lot of dirt, but the outcome was fabulous gold nuggets of community which changed all of our lives for the better.

I suggest you start your community development process by building your community with God. He longs to have a relationship with you. He longs to have you join in community with him. So start by setting aside a time each week to hang out with God. Go off alone. Find a place without distractions (kids, TV, computer, smart phone, iPad, bills…). Take the time to speak with God. Tell Him what you've been up to, what you are thinking, and how you are feeling. Get things off your chest that might be bothering you. Be honest, God can take it (oh, and he already knows what you are going to share). Take time to walk somewhere and experience nature and its beauty while appreciating God's creations. Find a spot to sit quietly and just listen. Wait to hear what God says to you. Soak in his glorious presence, and let him minister to you.

As you pray and seek friends, see if there is one person you can add to your time with God each week. Set aside a time to meet them. Get away from distractions and find a place you feel comfortable talking. Enjoy this time and each other's company. Share what's been going on in your life, what you are thinking, and what you may be feeling. Affirm and encourage each other as you share thoughts. It may be a good time to study something together--perhaps a devotional book, a book from the Bible, a book on a topic of spiritual interest. Finally, conclude by asking how you can pray for each other until you meet again. If you feel comfortable, pray for each other's requests before you depart.

When you get a second friend who may feel comfortable with sharing spiritual time, invite them to join your group. There may be fits and starts but eventually you will find that God is growing community around you. How do you know if what your group is doing is community? Quite simply, if the people in the group are growing in love and trust for each other, you individually and corporately are growing closer to God. That is what we refer to as community. It is an environment growing in caring, encouragement, and is a place where people feel safe to truly be themselves. The long-term goal is to build an environment of unconditional love and relationships that are not critical or judging and are accepting of differences. There is no magic formula that you should use in your small groups. Personally, I use the first third of the time sharing and getting to know each other. Then the next third is spent studying something that helps us grow in faith or the application of our faith. Finally we pray for needs in the group or the needs of others.

This process takes time, and you will hit speed bumps in the road, sometimes major speed bumps! As your relationships grow and deepen, you may get bored with each other or perhaps experience anger and frustration. Yes, people can be difficult, and they often are. Press on, hang in there, and work through the rough patches. Do not give up, and you will experience the fabulous fruit of deep, nurturing, and life changing community.

MANY TYPES OF COMMUNITY

Community is much like the people who make it up. They can be very different in appearance and approach. There is no one right answer. Let me give you some examples.

A few years ago, I was part of a community of two. Stu and I had been good friends for many years. He moved away and then met Jesus. It was hard to see each other because our work, social and family circles simply had no overlap. Finally we found a plan. I left home at 5:15 most Friday mornings to make the long drive an hour north. Stu drove south, and we met midway at Bill's Place, a classic greasy spoon diner. We both arrived at 6 AM when they opened. After an hour or more of great fellowship and sharing we would jump in our cars, roar off in separate directions to get to our jobs on time.

For many years I was part of a group of men who met every week in my hometown. The group was as small as two and at times had as many as ten. We had single guys, married guys, grandfathers, social workers, carpenters, college students, salesmen, retired pilots, and business executives. Our common bond was our desire to grow in our walk with Jesus. We met from 6 to 7 AM before everyone had to work. In the spring when landlocked salmon started to run in a local lake, we abandoned the study and meet on the dock to fish. Our community took place while fishing, talking, and drinking hot coffee. We took the summers off to be with our families.

Martie, my wife, has been part of a community which grew in her workplace. When she taught in a nearby elementary school, a student was hit and killed by a car one afternoon. The next day a handful of teachers who knew Jesus came to school early and prayed for the kids and families and teachers. This impromptu prayer session eventually became a regular group of female teachers that met in homes after school every Friday. They shared about life, faith, doubts, their marriages, and families. They invited seeking friends. They studied the Bible and other books. Many of Martie's teacher friends met Jesus in this community and grew to maturity in their walk of faith.

As a married couple, Martie and I have grown through small groups comprised of other married couples. People at the same ages / stages of life, often form good communities because their life circumstances are quite similar. For many years until we moved out of state, we were in a group of three to five couples plus an occasional single. We met every other week, usually on a weekday evening. (Most groups operate best with between six and twelve regular members. Less than six, if someone doesn't show up it can feel uncomfortably small. More than twelve and a number of people will stop sharing in the group.) My wife and I have been married for 30 years and have a strong relationship (we always win the "Newlywed Game" at parties because we have taken the time to learn a lot about each other). Yet Martie insists there is a part of me that comes out in a small group community that she would otherwise never get to see in our marriage.

"The Family," Larry and Joyce's community which I mentioned earlier, is more organized than most. They have had a membership of between six and sixteen adults plus kids over the 35 years of its existence. They meet on the first and third Tuesday of every month, although the schedule has varied over the years to accommodate the group's needs. Once a month they have a social activity. This could be as simple as a barbeque or a Christmas party or it could be more elaborate. One year they took 27 adults and kids to Disney World for a week. On another occasion they took a group of families to visit the historical sites in Williamsburg and Jamestown. Occasionally they meet on a weekend to do a service project (such as shingling a roof or painting a house) for someone they know who is in need. They rotate the meeting location between their homes and everyone takes a turn at hosting. They begin each meeting by sharing a potluck dinner together, and then they have a time with sharing, a study, and prayer.

Another powerful form of community is the "missional community." This is a group of people who come together not only out of a desire to grow spiritually but also out of a dedication to minister to a specific group of people or need. Years ago, I was part of a group of guys who were involved in an outreach ministry to the teens in our local high school. We rented a house together enhance our experience of community, but also to create a positive environment for the teens we were trying to serve. We met together one night each week and one Saturday morning a month to encourage and support one another. It was also easy to stay in touch and build friendships as we bumped into each other over breakfast or as we watched TV in the evening. The teens and our other friends were constantly dropping by and hanging out as our house gained a reputation as a warm and caring place.

Reba Place Fellowship is a community that started in the suburbs of Chicago. These people grew so close to one another, they bought some old houses, fixed them up, and moved in together. Each house might have several nuclear families, a couple or two and a few singles living in an intentional community together. The members of this community share a common fund, agree to live on the poverty level, and use their excess resources to minister to the needs of people afflicted by poverty in their neighborhood.

Michael Frost helped found a missional community dedicated to reaching out to the arts people in his neighborhood in Melbourne, Australia. His community consists of six to eight leaders who form the core of the group. They meet every Sunday night for a big community dinner, which might include up to 50 people at varying levels of commitment. The leadership team has made five lifestyle commitments as their covenant with the group:

1. **BLESSING:** A commitment to "bless" three people a week. This could be a phone call, a note of affirmation, or simply time spent together.
2. **EAT:** A commitment to eat a meal with three people outside your immediate family each week. Sunday night counts as one; Michael has breakfast each week with a group of guys, so he only needs one more to meet this goal.
3. **LISTEN:** Set aside one block of time per week to listen to God. Simply hang out with him and simply listen.
4. **LEARN:** Set aside one block of time each week to learn from God.
5. **SERVE:** A commitment to serve someone outside the community at least once a week.

This interesting set of community commitments (which goes by the acronym BELLS), allows a great deal of freedom to individuals in both their expression of a life of faith and in whom they connect with each week. At the same time, it offers those in the core a consistent set of spiritual practices which ensure both individuals and the group grow to be more like Jesus.

Recognize that real community is a work of the Holy Spirit. It's not a formula or methodology. There are lots of different ways God can create community. At the same time, you need to understand, not every small group has or is "community" in the Biblical sense. Some people in the Christian church feel any group or social gathering equals community. If four guys meet once a month to fly fish, that's community. If a group of ladies plays golf every Wednesday, that's community. Not exactly. The fact is, unless there are intentional efforts at spiritual nurture and Christ's mission built into the group, the activity will not produce people who are becoming more like Jesus. It is easy to have a warm social fellowship that has no spiritual benefit. Many people experience this very phenomenon when they go to their congregation on Sunday. They have been seeing these same people for years, yet they really don't know them. Nodding at the same people in the foyer year after year does not produce the quality of community God intends for Christ followers.

Biblical community has two hallmarks. First, it is a safe environment. The people in the group have to feel known and accepted before they can be honest and open. Eventually, this leads to unconditional love between the members. The second hallmark - whatever you do by way of content or process-- leads the members to grow spiritually, to become more like Jesus. All Biblical communities have an intentionality about growing with God.

Over the years I have discovered several other ingredients which may help your group transform itself into biblical community. **Sharing a meal** when you get together is one key ingredient. This is precisely the purpose of communion as Jesus and the Apostles shared it. Check out the New Testament passages. It was not a magical religious ceremony practiced together by a room full of strangers. It was a potluck, a family dinner which stretched over several hours and created bonds of love between the participants.

I recently learned of research which explains why the meal is so important. In the human body there is a special hormone which is only secreted in a limited number of situations. Oxytocin, also known as the "love hormone," is normally released during sexual intercourse, and it is present in both the mother and child during labor and birth. It also appears when the child is breastfeeding and "in other situations of love and altruism, for example, sharing a meal."[12]

Proximity is another element that helps build community. When people are in a group together and they find ways to encourage and support each other outside the regular group meeting, it accelerates the development of real community. It helps if you live in the same neighborhood and have multiple chances to interact during the week. Of course, your "neighborhood" might be work or the gym, but the point is to engage on several levels over a period of time and not just share a 90-minute bible study each week.

A few years ago a man came to consult with me about his small group. He told me they had been meeting every Friday night for bible study for 15 years, but the group had not yet gelled into community. As we talked, it became clear the members of the study had no other contact with each other during the week. "We come together to study God's Word Friday night, but if you had a tree down in your yard that needed to get cleaned up on Saturday, you would never think to ask the group for help," he related. "We just study the Bible. For anything else, you are on your own." This is a group that lacks proximity, and it's keeping them from community.

Shared common experiences can also help create powerful community. When group members share some kinds of experiences, it creates glue that holds people together. Veterans of war often feel this bond with foxhole buddies or members of dangerous professions such as police. If you have been on a short-term overseas mission trip with a group of people or been through an Alpha Program, it can create this tie. I saw this unique closeness among my mother-in-law's siblings. Raised on the mission field in India in the middle of the last century, they were shipped back to the States to attend college with nothing but a steamer trunk. All four married, raised their families, and had interesting careers – but they remained far closer that most families. Even their children had closer ties than most kids in nuclear families. Their unique shared experience created powerful bonds for a several lifetimes.

God is a creative God who delights in variety. There are probably as many ways to build community as there are different faces and personalities among people. I could fill an entire book with examples of effective communities I have seen among God's people around the world. It can happen with your rugby team. It can happen in a German beer garden. It can happen in a quiet flower garden in Sussex. God's creativity is not limited, so don't limit yours either.

Jesus wants us all to discover and grow from the rich spiritual environment provided by community. The next step is up to you. Take a step of faith, begin to pray and explore, and see what kind of community God creates for you.

Discussion Questions – Chapter 9

1) Did you meet anybody new this week? Tell us about that. How could you follow up and encourage the relationship?

2) Were you ever in a club or on a team when you were a child? How did that group make you feel?

3) Describe your reaction to this quote: "Life is about me."

4) Have you ever experienced real community with other believers during your walk of faith? Describe it.

5) Do you think modern communication technology helps people experience genuine friendship or does it actually keep people apart? Defend your answer.

6) Do you have any margins in your life which would allow you to invest in relationships with others? How much time could you carve out of your schedule each week?

7) Think about your own relational network – where do you find it easiest to be Jesus with skin on? Where is it hardest?

8) Are there people in your relational network you need to initiate with? What can you do in the next week or two?

Chapter 10 – Caring for the Poor

WWJD

"What Would Jesus Do?" reads the bracelet on millions of wrists across America. Over the past few years, many people, especially high school aged teens, have succumbed to the WWJD fad sweeping across America. Literally millions and millions of armbands as well as T-shirts, hats, jewelry and even tattoos have been sold promoting this slogan. What does it mean? Well, it depends on who you ask. For some it is an expression of faith in Jesus, for others it is a reminder to act like Christ in their daily circumstances, and for many it is simply an expression of cool, merely a fashion accessory.

Charles M. Sheldon first popularized this phrase in 1897 in a book entitled *In His Steps*. Sheldon, a reforming pastor, used this story to challenge his readers to respond to the poverty and suffering afflicting so many citizens of American society at the end of the 19th century. His point was that if the "haves" of society, especially those who know Jesus, would address the social ills of their day as the Jesus revealed in the Bible did, most of those problems could soon be eradicated.

One hundred years later it is clear Sheldon's challenge to those of us who are Christ followers is still relevant for the America we live in today. While the United States is the wealthiest nation in the world with one of the highest concentrations of Christians, we also have the highest rate of poverty of any industrialized democracy in the world. About 18% of our population, or 48 million people, live below the poverty line. Even with the help of Social Security almost one fourth of our elderly live in poverty.

By comparison, poverty in the United States is nearly twice as high as Canada and the United Kingdom and almost three times as high as that of many

European countries. Think about it. We are the wealthiest nation in the world. A vast proportion of our population claims to be Christian. We live in enormous houses. Many people battle obesity because of an excess of indulgent eating. Our government gives citizens a tax break to encourage the purchase of Hummers that weigh 5 tons and average less than 10 miles per gallon. Yet a huge proportion of our population lives as if in a third world country. What's with up that?

THE GOOD SAMARITAN

It seems obvious that somehow our beliefs about God, our beliefs about how we should treat other people, and what we actually do in our behavior have drifted perilously far apart. In the story of the Good Samaritan (Luke 10:25-38), Jesus tries to drive home the point that there is a very close connection between our faith in him and how we treat others. As Jesus tells the story, a minister, of high standing in the church with lots of external signs indicating his piety and godliness, comes across a stranger who has been mugged and robbed and left lying by the side of the road. He crosses to the opposite side of the road, averts his eyes, and hurries on. A seminary professor, with numerous advanced degrees in theology and other fields of knowledge, turns up but he too ignores the plight of the victim. Finally the Samaritan, the social equivalent of today's dirty, stinking, homeless wino, comes along and cares for the poor guy. Jesus concludes by spelling out that faith is not about religious accomplishment, it is not about knowledge and learning, it really comes down to how you treat others.

Somehow, it is all too easy for us to separate our faith beliefs from our behavior. We love God and delight in His goodness to us. We are grateful for His presence and answered prayer. We see that, just as He promised, Jesus provides for our needs. He is with us through the tough times and the sweet times of our lives. But then we forget to pass on these blessings we have been given to those who are around us. Jesus exhorts us not to let ourselves drift into this kind of spiritual schizophrenia. His teaching on this issue is practical and to the point. When preaching to the crowds convicted his listeners, and they asked what they should do, the reply was simple. "The person who has two coats should share with him who has none, and the person with food should do the same."

When I first started to take this teaching of Scripture to heart, I was puzzled as to how I was supposed to care for the poor. I didn't know any poor people. As far as I knew, we had no widows or orphans in our social set. Thanks to effective zoning laws, there were not any poor people in sight. Where was I supposed to find needy people to care for? Yet my heart's desire was to be obedient to Jesus.

When you don't know what else to do, it never hurts to pray. Martie and I started to pray. We asked Jesus to show us some poor people or to connect us to somebody we could help. A week later Martie got a call from someone down at our church. They said there was a young mother with a sick preschooler in the local hospital, would we go visit her? Hmmm…this is awkward. We did not know this woman. Neither of us was fond of visiting hospitals. The thought of calling on a stranger made us a little queasy. However, we went out of sheer dogged obedience.

At the hospital we met Diane and her 2-year-old daughter Janelle. The little girl had been sick for many weeks, had become dehydrated and soon she landed in the hospital. As soon as Janelle became sick, her father announced parenting was not for him and he left. Over the course of the next two years, we loved, encouraged, and supported Diane and her daughter as she went through a difficult divorce. We became family, and it seemed God grafted us into each other's lives. This single mom and her daughter had as much positive impact on our family as we did on theirs. It was clear to us of God's desire when He tells us to care for widows and orphans.

HEAD HEART HANDS

Here is the heart of the fifth spiritual discipline. Jesus wants to convince us that what we *do* with our faith is as important as what we *think* or *feel*. In fact he indicates that how we treat those who are less fortunate than ourselves will be a telling indication of who really has faith in Jesus and who is just giving him lip service. Truth be told, there is much about our relationship with Jesus that involves seeking balance. A mature faith in Christ involves "our head, our hearts and our hands." By that I mean that to grow in Jesus we must study his word, spend time getting to know him, learn all we can from the three persons of God. But we do not want to fall into the trap which has snared many of my fellow evangelicals, where our heads are stuffed with Biblical knowledge but we evidence little of the love and grace of Christ and we fail to lift a finger to help the needy around us.

We also want our hearts to grow. We all need to spend quality time with God, participate in worship, experience his love and catch his heart of passion for the lost world. But we do not want to succumb to an excess of emotion which ails some of my charismatic friends. This leads us to become totally caught up in feelings and experiences and never learn to know God or love others in a practical way. Finally, Scripture clearly teaches us that faith without works is dead (see James 2:14-26). How we treat others, especially the poor, is a strong indicator of a valid faith according to Jesus. What we do with our hands, our actions, our lives really matters. But we do not want to fall into the error of some of our mainline Christian friends, trying to live a life that consists solely of good deeds. Jesus wants us to grow in grace with a strong head, healthy heart, and active hands. All three disciplines lead to powerful and fruitful living in Christ.

Caring for the poor or for those less prosperous than ourselves is vital to learning and growing as a follower of Jesus. At the very beginning of his ministry here on earth, Jesus spelled out his *mission statement*, saying, "The Spirit of the Lord is on me, because he has anointed me to preach good news to the poor. He has sent me to proclaim freedom for the prisoners and recovery of sight for the blind, to release the oppressed, to proclaim the year of the Lord's favor." (Luke 4:18-19)

Jesus' mission becomes our mission when he goes to be at the side of his Father in heaven and leaves his ministry on earth to the Holy Spirit working through those who know and love him. Study the passage in Matthew 25:31-46. Jesus is teaching about how people will be sorted out for the final trip to heaven and hell. He says to those about to go to heaven, "When I was hungry you gave me something to eat, I was thirsty and you gave me something to drink, I was a stranger and you invited me in, I needed clothes and you clothed me, I was sick and you looked after me, I was in prison and you came to visit me." His hearers are incredulous and reply, "When did we ever see you hungry, thirsty, a stranger, naked, or a prisoner?" Jesus' reply highlights the principle underlying this spiritual discipline, "Whatever you did for the least of these, you did for me." The passage concludes with an address to those not going to heaven telling them that their neglect of the needy during their lifetime was essentially a neglect of Jesus himself. "Then they will go away to eternal punishment but the righteous to eternal life."

This is what Jesus would do, what he would have us do? When you are confronted with a need, see what you can do to help meet it. This is the powerful message Mother Theresa's life demonstrates. It began with caring for one dying woman on the street. Over 50 years this single expression of compassion for the needy grew into a ministry, which covers five continents, feeds 500,000 families, and cares for 90,000 lepers each year.

Mother Theresa's life demonstrates the power that is released when one person decides to take God at his word and obediently tries to meet the needs of those they encounter. It would be easy to dismiss what this one Catholic nun was able to achieve, as the story of an exceptional hero. Yet, I am not ready to do that. Now, I know God places different passions and different calls on each individual. This is how he weaves a tapestry into a big picture of the Kingdom, from all the individual and diverse people he created. I can't help but wonder if each of us could have the same degree of life changing impact, of world changing impact as this tiny Sister with a passion for the poor? What if you and I each gave ourselves whole-heartedly, without reservation, to our Kingdom mission, the Godly passion the Lord has planted in us from birth? Might we too be able to have this same world-changing impact for God?

THE POWER OF MONEY

What do we mean by caring for the poor? Who are the poor? Well, if you have a roof over your head, food on the table, and a car to drive, as do most Americans, you are already among the wealthiest 5% in the world. However, the poor are really all around us because the Biblical definition of the needy is not just a financial definition. Before we explore other types of needs that constitute a scriptural definition of poor, it would be helpful to see what the Bible teaches believers about money and wealth.

Jesus is not against money. He warns us against the destructive effect **the love of money** can have in our lives. The Book of Timothy puts it this way: "People who want to get rich fall into temptation and a trap and into many foolish and harmful desires that plunge men into ruin and destruction. For the love of money is a root of all kinds of evil." Jesus taught his disciples that money has a light side and a dark side. Money can be used to have a profoundly positive effect on the people and circumstances we encounter in life. It can be a source of much blessing and good. Jesus tells us to use our money wisely – to store up treasures in heaven by spending it on God's priorities. "For where your treasure is that is where your heart will be also."

Money also has a dark side. It's not that having money is bad; it's our attitude towards money that creates problems. The dark side of money is the belief that life is all about me. Money can reinforce that view and cause us to be self centered, selfish and focused on "What's in it for me?" Many people worry about having enough money, fear running out of money, and try to accumulate money or material possessions to make themselves feel secure and loved. This attitude leads to the bumper sticker I saw on a car, which read, "Whoever dies with the most toys wins!"

All of us struggle to some degree with the dark side of money. Someone asked one of the Rockefellers, who was worth about $5 billion at the time, "How much is enough?" His reply, "A little bit more." The dark side of money wants to convince us that we will never have enough and our future is in grave danger. We can't afford to be generous!

God can help us break the power of the dark side of money. He wants us to understand that our lives are in his hands and he is committed to taking good care of us. Life is not all about me! God can help us break the power of money and anxiety over our lives by giving some of our money away. That's right. The secret to being financially secure is to learn to give some of your money away. It's a paradox, but God has proven it true over and over again. God wants us to give away a portion of our money in recognition that he is the source of all our blessings and he wants to bless us more. We are needy and dependent in our relationship with God. He wants us to give to those in need who can be helped by our financial generosity in order that we might share in his ministry to those around us.

In the Old Testament era God established the pattern of having his people give 10% of their harvest to support the Temple, the priests, as an offering back to God. He specifically urged people to care for the widows and orphans as well as other needy people in their midst (Deut.14:29). This same principle of giving generously to God's work and the needs of those around you appears in the New Testament. "Whoever sows sparingly will reap sparingly, and whoever sows generously will reap generously." Take a look at this passage (2 Cor.9:6-11) and see how God promises that the more generous we are with the needy, the more richly will he supply our every need.

This Biblical concept (called tithing) is simply the practice of giving back and sharing with others. It is not a new form of legalism (although some people practice it that way). It is God's secret to releasing the light side of money in our lives. To quote Horace Van Der Gelder (from the movie *Hello Dolly*), "Money is like manure. Spread it around, and it will do a lot of good. Pile it up, and it just stinks." God wants us to learn to give generously so we can reap abundant blessings. In the Parable of the Talents (Matt.25:13-30), Jesus not only teaches that each of us will be held accountable for how wisely or poorly we invest the resources he gives us in life. He intimates that those who are good stewards of what we've been given will be given a whole lot more to manage for His sake.

SOWING GENEROUSLY

If you have never practiced giving back to others or tithing, let me suggest that it's ok to ease into it. Start with giving 2%. If you make $100 this week, set aside $2. If you make $1,000, set aside $20. Will that kill you? No, you probably spend more on than that fruffie coffee. If you manage your money on a monthly basis, pay your tithe first. If you pay it after all the bills are paid – you won't have anything left to give.

With time and experience, work gradually to build up your rate of giving and see how God blesses you. Giving to others sets him free to bless us. Some people ask 'should I give 10% of my gross pay or my net pay?' I really don't think it matters to God. He knows your heart and your financial circumstances. Remember, sow sparingly, reap sparingly. Personally, I aim for 10%, but feel free to give to special needs that come up over and above the 10%. There have been times when God has so blessed my finances that I was able to give away over 25% of my income. Let me tell you, giving will provide you with a real thrill and a sense that you are ministering to people and making a difference in the world.

I know one guy who takes ten percent of his pay each week and shoves it into a 2 ½ gallon glass pickle jar. He simply prays and when God shows him a person with a need, he digs into the jar and gives cash. Many people like to give to a church to support ministries that meet needs in the community. The Vineyard Church in Columbus, Ohio, has two boxes by the exit doors in their meeting place. One box collects funds to support ministries in the church. The other uses all the money placed in the box to meet needs of people who are not part of the church. Every month they provide a medical clinic, a car repair and replacement service, tutorial help for kids, and financial help for poor families from these funds.

If you participate regularly with a local church, feel free to direct the bulk of your giving through that church. If not, there are other Christian agencies that meet the needs of others and are worthy of your support. My kids have each sponsored third world orphans through Compassion International or World Vision. World Relief helps with global issues of poverty and starvation. Other agencies may do missions work overseas, or bring the Gospel to high school kids in your own neighborhood. There may be a soup kitchen or homeless shelter nearby that you can volunteer in.

Or you can just go do it yourself. I read a story about a 13-year-old boy in Philadelphia who became so concerned with the plight of the homeless during the holidays that he convinced his parents to donate every spare blanket in the house. Then he got his mom to drive him to 13th and Race Streets that night so he could personally hand out blankets to people on the street. After that he started collecting blankets from his neighbors, and it snowballed into a citywide effort to relive the plight of these people. What a great do-it-yourself ministry for a person of any age!

Some people will tell you that Scripture teaches a full 10% of your giving must go to the church you belong to before you give to anyone else. Actually, I would argue that the New Testament gives equal weight to a diversity of causes as the recipients of your generosity. A careful study of the Bible indicates that giving to meet the needs of the poor, widows and orphans is as important to God as supporting the ministries of your church. In my own titheing I give a regular monthly gift to my church but also to a half a dozen ministries in the USA and abroad. We also like to give books to local kids who need reading help or reading material. Martie's work in the school as a reading teacher puts her in touch with both situations of need and appropriate resources. Finally, we often give special financial gifts, over and above our tithe, to specific individuals we know who have a particular need.

It is important to invest some of your money in meeting the needs of less prosperous people we know personally. Don't just write a check to the Deacon's Fund or the Red Cross and say, "Great, now that's done." God may want to use our generosity to build a bridge to someone so they can discover the love of Jesus. I have friends who have struggled through unemployment, who have gotten cancer and can't work, whose income has been cut off due to the heart attack of the sole wage earner. I try to help out by sharing "extra food" that doesn't fit into my freezer. Sometimes I place an envelope with a couple hundred dollars in the back door. Occasionally I'll drop a bag of groceries off on the back steps when no one is around. When we have a garden, we practically become "vegetable evangelists" as we donate bags and bags of produce to people we think might enjoy them. Often older people don't so much need the vegetables as they simply appreciate being thought of and visited. Not only does this keep you from overdosing on zucchini and tomatoes, it's a great way to build relationships.

It's exciting to see how God can use generosity to build faith. A number of years ago, I was driving down the expressway on my way home, when the Lord spoke to me in that small still voice. "Send Jimmy Holiday $1,000." Immediately I shot back, "What, are you crazy???" I thought I must be hearing voices. God's response, "I want you to send Jimmy $1,000." Jimmy was a friend from college. I had not seen him for at least five years. I had the money, although it was 25% of my savings. It did not make any sense, but I was convinced it was what God wanted me to do. That night I put a check in the mail to Jimmy with a note telling him the Lord had asked me to send it to him.

A couple of days later Jimmy called to thank me, and I got the rest of the story. One of his little girls needed eye surgery. A struggling pastor of a small congregation, without health insurance, Jimmy scraped up every penny he could find, but he was still $1,000 short. So he got his wife and three kids around the kitchen table and they prayed. They asked God to send the money for Kara's operation. Two days later, my check showed up. God promises to provide.

THE MANY FACES OF NEED

Needs are not always simply a lack of financial resources. Les Gapay was a reporter for the *Wall Street Journal*. He was working as a freelance journalist in California when the dot com bust hit the economy. His work dried up, his savings consumed, Les ended up homeless – living in his truck in campgrounds just trying to survive until he found some work. What he needs is help finding work.[13]

Many of the homeless have similar stories. In the last year over 3 million Americans were homeless, about 30% of them chronically. Many of the homeless are single parent families. Jessica Lampman, 22, and her daughter Destinee, fled her mother's home to avoid the heavy drug use by her brother. She pitched a tent at a campground and got a job (20% of the homeless have full time jobs). Her low wages and poor credit history kept her from getting an apartment.[14] Intact families also slide into homelessness due to a job loss or health crisis. Researchers estimate that two out of every three wage earners in America are two paychecks from financial disaster. If something unexpected happened to their job or their health, in a month they would be in deep trouble. Just a few years ago, Hurricane Katrina and Rita roared through the Gulf coast and displaced over a million people from their homes and jobs. Many of these people were fine before the storm. Now they have lost everything, simply from a severe weather event, and it may be years before they ever recover, if they ever do.

When the US housing bubble collapsed in 2007 -2008, it drove the national rate of unemployment in America to a high of 10%. Another 7% were either underemployed or so frustrated that they've given up looking. If you total those who are unemployed, those who are underemployed, and those who are mis-employed (are in jobs that really don't fit or don't meet their basic needs), close to 40% of Americans continue to be involved in a full blown career crisis.

When Jesus encourages us to care for those who are less prosperous than ourselves, it may be a financial need, but the need can take many other forms. Some people may need help with a financial gift, or food, or shelter. But many other needs undermine people who we pass by every day. Loneliness, grief, illiteracy, depression, sickness, relational problems are some of the other faces of need. We might have to pray and open our eyes to see the need around us. Many times we simply tune out the genuine hurt of others, sometimes out of selfishness, but usually because we are too busy, or because we allow appearances to deceive us.

Wealthy people can be needy. Tamara DiMato was a wealthy divorcee, who bought and restored a beautiful home overlooking a large lake in Michigan. She entertained, traveled extensively, and seemed to have plenty of money. No problems, right? Actually, Tammy was a fairly new believer, and she had a lot of issues that kept her from growing with God. She struggled with trusting God after being abandoned by her husband. The dysfunctional family rules that had flourished in her bad marriage (don't talk, don't trust, don't feel) continued to influence and undermine her relationships with her adult children.

The divorce settlement meant that she had no worries about money, but she also had no purpose in life. There was no one who needed her, whose needs she was meeting. She had trouble forming friendships – whenever she got frustrated or bored she would take off on a trip for several weeks. Here is the classic picture of a needy person. She may not have money problems, but she needs a friend - someone who will take the time to listen, who will encourage her to grow in Christ and who will not be intimidated by her wealth.

You could have needy people at work. A teacher friend of ours told of a colleague who apparently was doing fine. Great family, active in her church, and active in community arts. One morning her husband drove to work early in the morning, fell asleep at the wheel, and was killed when his car went off the road and hit a tree. The grieving widow was left with three children to raise. Financially, between her husband's life insurance and her job as a high school biology teacher, the family's finances were ok. Other needs – the need to grieve her loss, caring for her high school and college-aged kids, the struggle to move on and make decisions about the future – all of these conspired to overwhelm this widow of 52. She needs practical help: a listening ear or wise counsel on decisions. Help with larger home repairs. Support in her parental role and responsibilities.

Carolee Fry is a single woman, a junior high teacher in Florida. In the course of her work she noticed one student in particular who seemed lost and in trouble. Loretta, she later learned, had been having a tough time. Her father died when she was one, and her mother died when she was 12. Now 14, she lived with her stepfather and was so unhappy she was drifting into a downward spiral of drinking and drugs to dull the pain. Miss Fry, as Loretta called her, gradually reached out and befriended this lost and lonely child. It began with Loretta calling on the phone to chat. Then there were occasions they went out for a bite to eat or went to school football games.

During this time Carolee kept sensing the Lord telling her, "Loretta really needs someone to care for her" but Carolee resisted. Finally one cold winter evening, she got a call from the hospital emergency room where Loretta had just been treated for severe bronchitis. "Can I come stay with you, Miss Fry?" she asked. "My stepdad won't take care of me like you will." Miss Fry's heart melted for this needy child. She nursed her through her illness. The following summer Loretta moved in with her, and she helped her kick the drugs and alcohol. A year later, her stepfather consented and gave Miss Fry custody. Eventually she adopted Loretta, who finished high school with good grades, and went on to finish college.[15]

Not all needs are as intensive as Loretta's. Some might only take an hour a week of your time to change a person's life for the better. Last week a good friend shared with me a story about new people she recently met at the local Department of Motor Vehicles. This couple had left New York City to drive to Philadelphia (about a four-hour drive) on Monday. It was now Thursday, and they were in Chambersburg, PA about three hours due west of Philadelphia asking for directions. They were completely frustrated, overwhelmed, and exhausted by their ordeal. Yes, there had been a small problem with a flat tire, but the basic issue was their inability to read well enough to follow the signage to their destination.

Can you imagine how hard life would be if it took four days to complete every four hour task because you could not read? The statistics indicate that 30% of American adults are not able to read and write well enough to handle a checking account. There are also many immigrants who need help learning the English language. There may be a program in your community that needs your help as a volunteer to help others become more competent in their language skills. Your small gift of time could change a person's life forever.

Practical help can fulfill this element of discipleship and may open other doors of friendship. One of my buddies loves to mow his lawn. He can't wait to hop on his riding mower and zip around his acre bringing his weed free lawn to manicured perfection. This spring he noticed his neighbor's lawn was looking a little shabby so he just cruised over and did her yard as well. The neighbor was a single mom, but Jack did not know her well. About the third time he mowed her lawn, she came out to thank him. It turns out her Mom had recently died, one of her kids had pneumonia, and her life was unraveling. Jack and Carol immediately rolled up their sleeves and got involved. Over the course of the summer, they not only were able to provide a lot of practical help, but they also developed a growing friendship with this neighbor.

Most of the kinds of caring we have surveyed in this chapter offer the opportunity to get to know people and to build friendships. I'm sure that's one of many reasons Jesus urges each of us to get involved in caring for the needy. Whether the person's need is financial, a health issue, a social need or an emotional problem – your willingness to reach out and help can open that person's spirit and heart to you. They may have more than a personal need. They may have a spiritual need as well.

Lots of our family, friends, and neighbors do not know Jesus. Often when we hit a limitation, when tragedy strikes or the unexpected floors us, that's when we do a personal check up and discover the emptiness of our spiritual condition. That has certainly been my experience. We hit the wall. We are at the end of the rope. We are pinned down and under attack by our circumstances and all the heavy fire life sometimes throws at us. We are not sure how to get in touch with God, but we are asking questions and ready to start searching. We recognize our spiritual need. Hopefully, we have a safe person in our life, someone we trust enough to be honest with so we can start to dialog and explore the issues of faith, which leads us to the last of the relational disciplines, sharing with the spiritually hungry.

<u>Discussion Questions – Chapter 10</u>

1) Do you know any of your neighbors? How well? How much do you know about their needs?

2) Love is as love does. How could you show the love of Jesus to a neighbor?

3) Are there practical ways you could reach out and help those who are less fortunate in your community?

4) Would you be willing to pray daily about the issues described in this chapter for the next week – to see what Jesus lays on your heart?

5) If you consider your faith as a balance between the head, the heart, and the hands – where do you place too much emphasis? Too little? What can you do about it?

6) Does money have a grip on your life? Have you ever experienced the release that comes from giving generously? Describe where you see yourself on this issue?

7) What unmet needs in your community has God put on your heart in the last year or so? What could you and your friends do to meet that need? Will you commit with them to take action?

8) Would your group / class take steps to do a service project together to meet a need in your community?

Chapter 11- Sharing with the Spiritually Hungry

ON THE OUTSIDE LOOKING IN

Do you remember what it was like to be on the outside looking in? Before you knew Jesus? When you were hungry, searching, and asking questions? The aching, the doubts, the sleepless nights? Looking at your life and feeling that somehow, the glass was half empty, you were missing something, and it could be important? Those of us who have come to faith as adults all have a conscious memory of some type of spiritual yearning.

Then, God turned on the lights. It happens in many different ways. For me, I had been searching for spiritual answers for years. I tried many alternatives but each ended in disappointment. Finally, I met a follower of Jesus who told me about the free gift of new life I could experience in Jesus. "Bruce, it's like this. You hold up the mirror and look at your life. If you like what you see, great! There is no problem. If you don't like what you see, you can give your whole life to Jesus. He will keep all the good bits, he will get rid of the bad stuff, and he will replace it with his good stuff." It took me a little while to get up the guts to "look in the mirror at my life." When I did, I stopped right where I was, knelt on the sidewalk on 23rd Street in Ocean City, New Jersey, and gave my life to Jesus.

Someone has said that sharing faith is like one hungry beggar who has found a source of free bread, telling the other beggars where they can find food. There was nothing in my life that made me deserving of Jesus' love and salvation. I was simply a starving beggar and an undeserving one at that. Jesus took pity on me and gave me grace and a new life in him. My friend Moffet took pity on me and told me about the free gift of salvation and new life she had received so that I could get in on the deal. Just one beggar telling another how to find free food.

GOD'S STRATEGY – JESUS WITH SKIN ON

This is the heart of the last spiritual discipline: Learning to share with the spiritually hungry. Our world is full of people who are starving to death spiritually. In the United States the proportion of people who don't know Jesus is quite high. If you live in the "Bible Belt," half the people you know are spiritually lost. In other sections of the country, perhaps nine out of ten of our family and friends go to bed spiritually hungry each night. How does God feel about this? Jesus tells us, "Your Father in heaven is not willing that any of these little ones should be lost." (Matthew 18:14) The Father's deepest desire is that every one of his lost children comes to faith and joins the Forever Family.

Many of the spiritually hungry are deeply concerned about their spiritual health. Sometimes we believers get shy when it comes to talking to family and friends about our faith, especially if we've only known Jesus for a short time. The thought runs through our head, "What if they think I'm crazy, like I'm talking to ghosts or something!" In truth there is widespread interest in God and spiritual things among people who appear to be quite secular. American universities have recently discovered this. A survey of 100,000 college freshmen found four in five (80%) reporting an interest in spirituality, with three in four (75%) searching for meaning or purpose in life. The vast majority (80%) of these seekers say they want to discuss religion and spirituality with friends. The Gallup Organization recently polled a national cross-section of adults and found a similar proportion (about 80%) who were open to discussing spiritual issues.

This is where believers come in. God's plan to reach the spiritually lost is simple. His plan: over the course of our lifetime, we each would introduce a handful of friends to Jesus. This is God's incarnational strategy. Incarnation means "in the flesh." Jesus is the first part of the incarnational strategy – He is all of God in a completely human form. The Father sent Jesus into history and our world because we could identify with him and relate to him. Now the Holy Spirit lives in each of us so we can be God's incarnation here on earth. Why? For the same reason – our family and friends can identify with us. This is the second part of His strategy. As we go about our everyday life, we are to be His hands and feet to do His work in this world. We are literally to become "Jesus with skin on," Jesus in the flesh, to our family and friends who don't yet know Him.

The transition from Stage 1 to Stage 2 of God's strategy is given to us by Jesus in Matthew 28:18-20. He's gathered his disciples for his last instructions before he ascends to heaven to be with his Father. He tells the disciples he has been given all authority in heaven and earth and now. "This is what I want you to do: as you go out into the world and go about your life, make disciples of all peoples, baptizing them in the name of the Father and of the Son and of the Holy Spirit, and teaching them to obey everything I have commanded you."

Some believers make the mistake of thinking the job of sharing of faith is for the church, pastors, specialists, or big events. A careful study of Scripture will lead you to conclude that spreading the word about our source of spiritual food is a responsibility of all believers. In spite of this clear teaching, there remains a lot of confusion about this issue in some Christian circles. Jesus has given us a pretty good principle to determine what we are supposed to do to share faith. In John 15 he says that what glorifies God is that we bear much fruit and that when we do so, we show the world that we are his disciples. So let's ask the question; which methods of sharing faith produce followers of Jesus? In other words, which methods produce spiritual fruit?

How do people in America actually come to faith? In a research study [16] among 10,000 believers respondents were asked, "What was responsible for your coming to Christ?" Their answers:

An evangelistic crusade	½ of 1%	A program / event	3%
Home visitation	1%	Sunday school	5%
A special need	2%	Pastor	6%
Came to church on my own	3%	A Friend / relative	79%

The facts show that four out of five people come to faith by a friendship with a peer. Not a religious professional, a church program, or a special event. Instead, a friend or family member, much like you or me, loves them and introduces them to Jesus.

Yolanda Adams tells of her difficult childhood growing up in a rural town in southern California. Her tattered clothes, poor hygiene, and her family situation all made her the butt of unmerciful taunts and verbal abuse at school. Much to her amazement, two of her classmates decided they were going to be her friends. They walked to school with her, included her in games on the playground, protected her from bullies, and even encouraged her when she had hard things happened at home. Eventually Debbie and Terrie invited Yolanda to attend church with their families. Much of what went on in church made no sense to her. "Then one Sunday the children's sermon really spoke to me," Yolanda recalls. "Jesus loves you. You don't have to be perfect. He won't give up on you, no matter what." Just like Debbie and Terrie had been there for her. She gave her heart to Jesus and has been growing with him ever since.[17]

Billy Graham has been the most effective evangelist in the history of the world. We are grateful to God for all he's been able to do through this man and his ministry. But let us suppose the Graham organization could reach a million people a year for Christ. (In fact, ten years ago when Dr. Graham was in better health, they reached about 150,000 people in the United States each year. But we will be generous and round that up to a million.) At that rate it would take the Graham Crusade 200 years to reach all of the lost in America, if no one else was born and no one dies! By contrast, look at the effectiveness of God's incarnational strategy. If every believer in America introduced two or three friends to Jesus over their lifetime, it would take one generation, less than 40 years, to reach all of the lost in America.

TWO WAYS TO SHARE FAITH

There are two ways God uses His people to share Jesus with spiritually hungry people. Witnessing is a method God uses to reach people in an everyday way, especially those who have some relational contact with Christians. Witnessing is the role and responsibility of every believer. The Apostle Peter said, "Always be prepared to give an answer to everyone who asks you to give the reason for the hope that you have." (I Peter 3:15)

Evangelism is a spiritual gift given to a few believers to reach people in special circumstances – especially those who have no contact at all with followers of Jesus. Research indicates only about one out of ten in the Body of Christ have this spiritual gift. How do you know if you have the spiritual gift of evangelism? If you have it, you will have a burning desire to tell people you meet, even complete strangers about Jesus. Like other spiritual gifts, one sure sign you have it is fruitfulness. If you have ever sat down on an airplane or a bus and led a complete stranger to Christ before you got to your destination, you probably have the gift. I watched a friend get on a ski lift with a stranger and lead him to faith before they got off at the top – that's the gift of evangelism at work.

The problems most believers have experienced with sharing their faith comes from the confusion between witnessing and evangelism. Most of the books and courses written on evangelism or sharing your faith are written by people who have the spiritual gift of evangelism. They think anyone can do or even *should do* what God has gifted them to do. It's not true. Study the three main passages on spiritual gifts – 1Corinthians 12, Ephesians 4, Romans 8. The Bible is clear –if you don't have the gift, you won't be fruitful in the same way as the person who does. That means, for nine out of ten believers, every time you try evangelism methods, you stand a pretty good chance of having it fail.

What we call "lifestyle witnessing" is very different than evangelism methods. Any believer can do it. You don't need to have a particular spiritual gift; in fact God has designed witnessing to fit the gift you have been given. It's relaxed. It feels more like you are being you. It feels more like having a friendship instead of having a debate. If you have tried some of these evangelism methods and they feel contrived or forced, almost like you are trying to trick someone into the Kingdom, it's probably because you are using evangelism tools, but you don't have the spiritual gift of evangelism.

DON'T EVANGELIZE WITHOUT THE GIFT

If God has not given you the spiritual gift of evangelism, he does not expect you to evangelize. I realize in saying this I am challenging the practices of many in the American church. According to their teaching, everyone should be involved in confrontational evangelism. "Just button hole any stranger any time or place you can and talk him through the four steps in this booklet." If you have the spiritual gift of evangelism, this approach may work for you. If you don't, it will just create pain and heartache for all who are involved. It may even drive people further away from God.

Let me explain it by using a word picture. Say you had a single friend who wanted to get married. Would you suggest the following strategy for finding a mate? "Go down to the nearest mall. Look around until you see a person of the opposite sex who seems reasonably attractive. Walk up to them and say, 'Excuse me, are you married?' If they say, 'No,' you say, 'Will you marry me?'

You probably would not recommend that as a strategy for finding a spouse. Instead you tell them to meet somebody, and then get to know him or her. Do some things together and build a foundation of common experiences. Talk and listen to each other. Give it time so mutual trust can develop. Finally, after some significant investment in knowing and being known, then you might want to pop the question.

If we generally don't marry strangers, what makes us think people will be open to a complete stranger knocking on our door or ambushing us in front of the grocery store, and then asking us to make a commitment far more profound than marriage? People simply do not want to open up about spiritual issues with a stranger. Remember the university research? It said people want to "discuss spiritual issues **with friends**." Unless God has gifted us with the spiritual gift of evangelism, which enables us to work outside the natural realm for God's purposes, we have to build a friendship and earn the right to discuss spiritual issues. This is the heart of lifestyle witnessing.

IT'S A PROCESS, NOT AN ENCOUNTER

Biblical witnessing is a process, not an encounter. Witnessing involves being a friend, and real friendships take time to develop. It takes time to see the fruit. It's a natural process Jesus has designed so we can go through life and intentionally focus on a few people God has put in our vicinity as we walk down the path of life. If you have tried some evangelism methods and had a painfully bad experience, let it go. God wants you to witness rather than evangelize, and he has designed the process so it fits, it feels like you are being you, it feels like you are being you with Jesus by your side as you love a friend. God, in his time and in his way, will use that process to allow you the privilege of introducing your family and friends to Jesus.

One of my daughter's college friends grew up in a wealthy, privileged home but without any faith. As a high school student, Patrick relates, "I felt all alone. My life was full of depression, anxiety, Zoloft, loneliness, and stress disorders. When I was at my loneliest, a Christian family took me in. They let me eat at their dinner table; they let me nap at their house. I was free to just hang around. We played board games together. It was nothing spectacular that led me to the Lord. This family saw I was lonely and hurting. They invited me to come over and hang out after school. In time I just wanted what made them that way. So that's how I came to know Jesus."

This is exactly the strategy Jesus demonstrated in His life here on earth. The great majority of His time in his public ministry was invested in building friendships with 12 guys. They worked together, ate together, traveled together, vacationed together, and generally hung out - experiencing life, while reflecting and talking it over. You see, even with Jesus, much of the spiritual life was "caught rather than taught." The most powerful way to share faith is by an intentional sharing of your life.

BEING AN EFFECTIVE WITNESS

Lifestyle witnessing is an intentional choice. It begins when you seek God's heart for the lost in your world, and your heart begins to resonate with his love for his lost children. Prayer is the process where we present ourselves to God and ask him to begin to give us a heart for his children. Think about how you would feel if your son or daughter wandered away from home and went missing. You would not rest easy even if police and neighbors were scouring the woods – you would insist on doing more. Even when everyone else gives up, a parent's heart keeps looking and hoping and waiting expectantly for the return of their child. That's how God feels about every one of his lost children.

Witness begins with a commitment to pray for God's heart for the lost and then moves on to pray specifically about the people God has placed in your world. In His divine wisdom God has placed you right where you need to be to be "Jesus with skin on" to someone in your circle of friends. You don't have to knock on doors, or go to the inner city, or travel overseas to find a mission field. God has given each one of us a personal mission field, and they are not strangers. They are people we already know. Yet, it is critically important that we pray and ask the Lord whom we should focus on. We are limited creatures. You can probably only build friendships of spiritual potential with one, two or three people at a time.

Only God knows the heart condition of each of those people in your life, and He can guide us to people who are seeking him.

As you pray, inventory the people that you know. It would be good to repeat the relational network exercise we did in Chapter 9. List the people you see daily, occasionally, and infrequently. Pray and ask God which of these people should be on your short list with whom you focus on building intentional friendships. Look for the same characteristics we looked for in seeking community. Ask if they are open and teachable, if they are available and if there is mutual affinity. Another factor is if you have ever discussed spiritual things with any of these people. Keep praying until God shows you whom to focus on.

I call this short list my *Impact List* and keep it in my shirt pocket so I can pull it out and pray for these people throughout the day. What do I pray for? I pray that God will create opportunities for me to reach out and be a friend to this person. I pray that God will give me his grace and words in caring for this person so I truly am "Jesus with skin on" in their life. I pray that God will reach out and increase their spiritual hunger and thirst. I pray that He will bring other people and circumstances into their lives that point them to Jesus. Finally, I pray he will deepen our trust and friendship to the point that we can have spiritual conversations.

REAL RELATIONSHIPS

Daryl was a client I had worked with in my business life. After several years, it dawned on me he might be a person God wanted me to befriend. So he went on my Impact List, and I started to pray. We had lots of chances to be together through business. We also invited each other into our social worlds. I got to know his friends, his family, and his love for wooden boats. He met Martie and the girls, and I'm sure he marveled at my recreations - fly fishing, fox trapping, and bow hunting. To be honest, after a couple years I thought, "This is never going to work. He simply has no need for God. A single guy with a Masters degree from Harvard, a great paying job, a lot of professional success, plenty of women friends, a hot car, and a good cigar... what would ever make him feel a need for God?" God simply said, "Be his friend."

Then Daryl got married. By the time he and Tina married they were both 36 and a lot of their friends were getting divorced. Daryl came to me, and we talked a lot about God's principles for a healthy marriage. They had a daughter and Daryl said, "I don't want to be the kind of Dad my father was, teach me God's perspectives on fatherhood." Then they lost two children before birth. Daryl was crushed. "Where is Jack and will I ever get to know him?" Our spiritual conversations grew deeper and happened more often. Finally, one day Daryl came to me and observed, "My life is great in so many ways. The glass should be 7/8ths full. Why does it feel half empty?" A few more conversations and a week later he gave his life to Jesus. This was six years after I started to pray.

It's a process. Developing friendships with spiritual potential takes time and some hard work. It may get messy, and it may force you to leave your comfort zone. It's like being a mom with a baby – lots of listening and caring and cleaning up messes. There are many small steps of growth and progress. It's not a project. If your friend ever feels like you have an agenda for their life, that you see them as a potential scalp to hang on your spiritual belt, they will disappear in a hurry. You need to be a safe person. Not judgmental and one who respects confidences. You need to be transparent, and open about your own life. We are all sinners and fail regularly. But we are forgiven and empowered by the Holy Spirit. They need to see you as a real person before they will accept your witness.

Love is practical. Look for things you have in common. Invite them into your life to share things you like to do. Ask them to teach you how to do things they like to do. Go out for a meal or invite them over to flip burgers on the grill. Look for ways you can serve them – shovel the snow, rake the leaves, take their kids for the evening. Asking them to help you will deepen the relationship. When we ask others to help us, it says we trust them and consider them true friends. Keep building your friendship until you have earned their trust.

How do you know if there is trust in your relationship? Think about your conversations when you are together. Gary Smalley says there are five levels of communication. The first three he calls "Normal Conversation." **Clichés** are safe and innocuous. "How about this great fall weather?" **Facts** are still safe, but somewhat more revealing. "I went fly fishing in Alaska last summer." **Opinions** are a little more risky. Remember when George H.W. Bush said, "I don't like broccoli?" He took a beating for expressing an opinion. He wasn't telling kids not to eat their vegetables or attacking the Broccoli Growers of America. He just said here is one vegetable, personally, he'd prefer to take a pass on.

The truth is many relationships, even many marriages, never progress beyond normal communication. There are two deeper levels of sharing, which Smalley calls Trust Communication. The fourth level is when you are able to **share how you feel**. "I'm afraid I'm going to lose my job and my wife will leave me, and I'll never see my kids again." It takes guts to share at this level. And no small amount of trust in the other person. Finally, when you can tell the other person **what you need**, that's the deepest level of communication. When I say to my wife, "Tell me what would make our marriage a 10 for you?" then I'm operating at Level 5 communication, the deepest level of trust.

STARTING SPIRITUAL CONVERSATIONS

Life is full of teachable moments. Ben & Amy Coggins met in college. Ben's mom had a strong walk with Jesus. He went to church with her as a kid. When he was in high school, he was in the church youth group, and the pastor's son was his best friend. On a cognitive level, he knew all about faith but was not interested. In college he rapidly moved into drinking, parties, and all kinds of wild behavior. He met Amy in his junior year. He tried to clean up his act, but they both still ran with a pretty fast crowd. Then Amy's mom died. She was 46 and healthy one day. The next day she was diagnosed with a Stage 4 cancer and died within three months. Amy's mom had a strong faith and encouraged Ben and Amy to accept Jesus before she died. Once she was gone, Amy realized that if her mom was going to spend eternity with Jesus, she wanted to be with her. She gave her life to God. It occurred to Ben, if that's where Amy was going, he wanted to be there with her. After decades of resistance, he finally gave his life to Christ.

As you go through life and as the trust in your friendship deepens, people encounter a wide variety of teachable moments. A close friend is killed in an auto accident. A marriage begins to suffer from tensions and problems. Unexpectedly a job is lost. Someone suffers from a health crisis. A child is headed in the wrong direction. You find yourself in a dead end job or career. In everyone's life, at some time or in some way…Stuff Happens.

When stuff happens to either you or a friend, this is a great time to start a spiritual conversation. Asking a question is a good way to start. You are standing in line at the viewing, and you say to your friend, "Do you ever think about what happens when we die?" Or, "I can't believe it. She was so young. How do you expect your life will play out? Do you ever wonder if there is life beyond this world?"

You don't have to wait for a crisis. Lots of conversations can lead to spiritual dialog. I was having lunch with two banker friends who, like myself, grew up in the Woodstock era. One of them commented, "Remember when we thought the answer to all of life's questions had to be 'Sex, Drugs, and Rock and Roll?'" I laughed and said, "Ok, but now that we've all had a lot more experience with life, have you thought about what the answers might really be?"

If your relationship is open and transparent, this will lead to spiritual conversation. When I share about my life, I talk a lot about my relationship with my wife, Martie, and my girls. They are central to all I do and who I am. Likewise, I talk about what I'm learning from God, how Jesus makes a difference in my life, and what the Holy Spirit is saying to me. It's who I am. When these topics come up you can ask directly, "Where do you think you are on your spiritual journey?"

Sometimes inviting a friend to share in a Christian resource can meet a common need. You are chatting at the health club and your friend mentions he and his wife are struggling with credit card debt. "We are too," you reply and invite them to attend a financial seminar at a local church, or a seminar on marriage, or one on raising kids. All couples going through these life stages struggle with similar issues. Taking them to a Christian seminar may give them both practical help and the opportunity to talk about spiritual issues.

Finally, offering to pray is a great door opener. I'm talking to a friend who mentions a pressing personal need in his life. I'll ask, "Would you mind if I prayed about that for you?" I've never had anyone turn me down. I then ask, "How can I pray for that need so that if God answers that prayer, you will know he did it?" I let them define the terms of the encounter. It's great. More often than not, a week later I'll get an excited phone call from my friend. "You won't believe it!" he will exclaim. "God answered your prayer for me!!!" He then will go on and share the details of what he is now defining as God's intervention in his life.

LEARNING TO TELL YOUR STORY

When you go into a court of law as a witness, there are certain rules that govern your testimony. As a witness, you are asked to talk about your own personal experience in the matter at hand. You can't talk about what some other person saw or said, that's hearsay evidence and it is not admissible. When Scripture commands us to be prepared to give a reason for the hope within us (1 Peter 3:15), our role as a witness for Christ is to simply tell our own story.

Our story of faith is of great interest to our friends, even if they don't know Jesus. Our friends are interested because it involves us. If they are willing to listen to your story about flying to France for the summer to explore the great vineyards, why wouldn't they want to hear about your adventures in faith? The second reason they are interested is because they can probably relate to it. It's likely you have a number of things in common (that's why you are friends) so the issues faith addresses in your life are potentially issues they have as well. Lastly, it's hard to argue with. It's not theology or dogma; it's your experience.

I recently heard Winifred Gallagher, an author and journalist; tell her story on a PBS special. "As a little girl, I had very powerful experiences of God's presence. Then I went to college at the University of Pennsylvania. By Thanksgiving of my freshman year, I was an atheist. Exposure to the scientific worldview had that much impact on me. At a certain point I began to do Buddhist meditation, because Buddhism is a non-theistic religion. Ironically, when sitting on my little cushion trying to keep my mind blank, I found myself back in contact with God. What I was experiencing was so authentic, so real, that I knew I was experiencing the Divine Presence."[18] This is a wonderful example of candidly telling your story.

This is probably something you will need to work on. When the opportunity arises, you want to be able to tell your story, clearly, confidently in five minutes or less. This may take some preparation and practice. Your story does not have to be dramatic or flashy. It simply needs to answer the question, "What difference does knowing Jesus make in your life?" Keep it fresh and current. Be real. Make it relevant to your listener. Make it easy to understand. Don't use Christian jargon or buzz words. Don't try to explain theology. You don't need a Bible verse for everything you share. Remember to relax. This is your story; it should sound a lot like you!

Take time and sit down with paper and pen to work this up. Then practice it on your own. Next try it out on a trusted friend. Ask for ways to improve it and make it easier to understand. Refine and improve it. Practice it some more, until you are really comfortable sharing it, and you can actually do it in five minutes. I love taking a seeker friend to lunch and saying, "Hey, I'm working on this course, and I have to learn to tell my story of faith. It's only five minutes. Could I practice it on you?" I've rarely been turned down.

So I share my story and then I ask the follow up questions I would ask any friend after sharing it. "Does this make any sense to you? Was there anything I said that was confusing? May I explain more? How do you feel about this? Would you like to know more?" If there is any degree of trust in your relationship, this is going to start a spiritual conversation. Big time.

SHARING THE GOSPEL

In addition to being comfortable telling your story, an effective witness needs to be able to share the Gospel clearly and in five minutes or less. Now "the Gospel" is a term much bandied about, but in the New Testament it simply means the "Good News." Sometimes believers get confused with all the spiritual truths they have been learning and all the information about God in the Bible. They are not sure what to share and what to leave out. Others think there is some magic set of formulas or beliefs that will lead a person to faith. "100 Easy Steps to Jesus." Ouch! It's a tough question - What to share, what to leave in, what to leave out?

When you boil everything in Scripture down to a few key issues, the first thing that becomes clear is that **the Gospel is the person of Jesus.** He is our means of forgiveness and is able to restore our relationship with God. He is our power for living, and our guide into eternal life. When we talk about sharing the Gospel, what we mean is that we want to give enough information and explanation so someone can put their hand in Jesus' hand and trust him to lead them the rest of the way.

Now I know you probably do not have the gift of evangelism. Neither do I! But we need to be able to explain how to have a relationship with God, so if God calls us to step into a situation we can help out. What if you are driving down the road, and there is a terrible wreck. You jump out to see if you can help. A young girl is lying in the ditch battered and bleeding and obviously headed for death. She reaches out, takes hold of your hand and pleads, "Tell me what I have to do to get right with God?" What are you going to say?

The Gospel, a basic explanation of how we trust ourselves to Jesus, is not that complex. The simplest version I've heard was taught to me by one of my daughters when she was in middle school:

1) God is holy.
2) People are sinful.
3) Christ is the answer.
4) What are you going to do about it?"

The Gospel is simple. Try to keep it that way. You can elaborate on it somewhat and make it your own. Here is how I might explain it:

1) God made us for relationship with him, but he is holy.
2) We broke the relationship and the consequence is separation: death.
3) Jesus died for our sins and created a way back into relationship with God. It's a free gift and all we have to do is accept it and act on it.
4) What are you going to do about it?

There are a lot of helpful ways to present the Gospel to introduce people to Jesus. I'm not going to repeat them here. There are additional resources on this in the Appendix. Simply find a way that works for you--one that you are comfortable with. You should be able to do it in five minutes or less, and you should be able to do it free hand, without props, or tracts. You want to be natural and relaxed. It's just another part of who you are.

OUR JOB vs. GOD'S JOB

What's the most important thing to remember about introducing a friend to Jesus? It's not about you and what you do. Let me repeat that: It's not about you! It's not about what you say or do! The Holy Spirit does all the heavy lifting in the process of redemption. We are simply bit players who have a small role in what God is doing. Often, you and I get confused about what our job is and what God does in the process. *Hear me loud and clear – you can't argue anyone into heaven.* Please don't try. It's not our job, and it will simply get in the way of what God is trying to do.

The role of the Holy Spirit in the process of redemption, according to Jesus, is to convict, to convince, and to judge. (John 16:9-11) "He works to bring us the conviction of sin, the recognition of the need for righteousness, and an awareness of impending judgment long before we come to the point of conversion and surrendering our life to Jesus Christ."[19] The Holy Spirit's job is to speak to our hearts in a language we understand, to pursue us, to convince us of the reality of Jesus and to finally enable us to take that step of faith to give ourselves to Jesus and trust him.

What's our job in the process? It's to love that person like Jesus would love them. We are to pray, to be a friend, to be a safe person. Our relationship is the best way to demonstrate what trusting Jesus looks like in a contemporary life – we are an "in the flesh" example of following Jesus that our friend can learn from. We need to inform as best we can – by sharing our own experiences, by telling our story and by sharing the Gospel. The Holy Spirit will do the rest. Be patient, he has his timetable, and he knows what he's doing.

When our daughter Katybeth was a college freshman in Virginia, she received an email from a high school friend. She was so concerned she called to ask us to pray for Penny who was at the University of New Hampshire near where we lived. She was depressed, unhappy and so down on herself, Katybeth was afraid she might hurt herself. That very day I had read in the **Boston Globe** about a UNH freshman who had committed suicide by throwing herself out of her 6th floor dorm window. In a panic, I picked up the phone and called Penny and invited her out to dinner.

Penny had been through some really traumatic life experiences. She was still the victim of a number of bad circumstances. We didn't know what to do for her. So we just tried to befriend her, and we prayed. We sent her email and notes of encouragement. Every other month we would go down and take her out to dinner. We stopped and visited with her on her summer jobs. We invited her home for holidays. We talked, and we listened. But Penny had so many issues and demons she was fighting. If you had asked me for a list of the last five people in the world who would ever accept Christ, Penny would have made the list. Yet, God in his love pursued her. About five months after her graduation, Penny met Jesus and began the wonderful journey of faith.

MAKING THE INTRODUCTION

When you sense your friend may be ready to trust Jesus, it's appropriate to ask a few leading questions. "Have you come to the point of trusting Jesus or are you still in the process of thinking it through?" "Where would you say you are right now in that process?" "Is there any reason you wouldn't want to ask God for his forgiveness and leadership right now?"

If your friend is ready, you can lead them to pray a simple prayer with you. For example, you can pray, *"Dear God, I admit I have sinned and fallen short and that I am separated from you. I want to accept the free gift of life in Jesus. I put my life in your hands and trust you as my Savior. Thank you for loving me and for giving me the gift of new life – both now and forever. I pray this in Jesus' name, Amen."*

Not everyone reacts the same way when they meet Jesus. My friend Reggie (Chapter 4) had "an overwhelming sense of peace and that I was no longer alone." Another friend's seven-year-old daughter had a similar reaction. "Now I will never be alone." Some people are overwhelmed by God's presence, while others like myself, feel no discernable change. Just assure your friend that they took a step of faith, and God will honor that. It's not how you feel, but that you trust Jesus. Feelings come and feelings go. As we will discuss in the next chapter, faith is based upon the factual reality of God and His promises. Celebrate their commitment and their new life in Christ.

At this point the journey is not over. In fact it has just begun. You need to keep caring for your friend. They are like a newborn baby – needing lots of time and attention. Continue to love them and build your friendship. Continue your spiritual conversations and answer their questions. You might suggest the two of you study the teachings of Jesus together, perhaps by studying the Gospel of John. You might take them through this book, or *Exploring God Without Getting Religious*, as an introduction to the basics of the faith. When they seem ready and are asking for more, invite them into your community. Have them attend your small group or perhaps some appropriate activity at church. Continue to pray for them and love them as they grow in Christ. Our long-term goal is to teach and encourage them until they are able to pass the faith on to others (see 2 Timothy 2:2).

Discussion Questions – Chapter 11

1) Briefly tell your own story of coming to faith. Keep it to 2 or 3 minutes.

2) Were you surprised by the statistics about how people actually come to faith? How did your view differ before you read this chapter?

3) How do you feel about evangelism – do you think you have the spiritual gift of evangelism? Why or why not?

4) Was there a part of the reading in this chapter that was particularly helpful for you, that made a connection in your mind, or that you disagree with? Share about your reaction to the difference between witnessing and evangelism.

5) How many current friendships do you have with pre-Christian people?

6) In your view, what makes a friendship? How do you tell who is a friend and who is just an acquaintance?

7) Have you ever had a spiritual conversation with a pre-Christian? How did that go?

8) How might you use what you learned in this chapter to change your life in the coming week or months?

Growing with God

Chapter 12 - Is Jesus Enough?

ONE ROCK AT A TIME

Over the course of the last six chapters, we have explored the basic disciplines that will help you grow in your relationship with God. As you work on implementing these personal and relational disciplines into your life, you will become aware that you are walking in step with Jesus and gradually becoming more like him. It's important to understand these are individual disciplines. No one else can do them for you.

My friend Stu says building faith is like the stonewall he is building in his back yard. Every time he finds some good rocks on the side of the road, he picks a few up and brings them home to dump in his back yard. Then stone by stone, he painstakingly fits them in, one at a time until a part of the wall begins to take shape. "Sometimes I think it would be easier to call up somebody, have them dump a huge pile of stone in my yard and come and make it into a wall while I'm off at work. But then, it wouldn't really be my wall, would it?"

Stu continued, "Building my faith is just like building that wall. I have to struggle to study the Bible on my own. I have to struggle to find time for God every day and to be available to the people he puts in my life. Sometimes I think, 'Wouldn't it be easier to go to church and have them tell me what to do?' Then I realize that if I want a faith that is mine, there are no easy answers. I can't get anybody else to do it for me. I have to build it myself, stone upon stone."

Jesus affirms this when he tells his disciples, "If anyone would come after me, he must deny himself and take up his cross daily and follow me. For whoever wants to save his life will lose it, but whoever loses his life for me will save it. What good is it for a man to gain the whole world, and yet lose or forfeit his very soul? (Luke 9:23-25). Our Lord is trying to communicate that our spiritual life will reflect the investments we make in it. If we drift along and do little, we will end up with a weak, shaky faith. If we consistently work on the spiritual disciplines, we will find our lives rich, vibrant and strong.

I also have to tell you, there is a test coming. Not just a pop quiz, but a serious, heavy duty, tough examination. Each of us will experience trials and testing, temptation and perhaps tragedy in our lives. Knowing Jesus does not insulate us from these events. But he does promise to go with us as we walk through them. Jesus tells us, "Everyone who hears these words of mine and puts them into practice is like a wise man who built his house on the rock. The rain came down, the streams rose, and the winds blew and beat against that house; yet it did not fall, because it had its foundation on the rock. But everyone who hears these words of mine and does not put them into practice is like a foolish man who built his house on sand. The rain came down, the streams rose, and the winds blew and beat against that house, and it fell with a great crash." (Matthew 7:24-27)

WHAT ABOUT CHURCH?

If the spiritual disciplines we've been exploring are individual, and we should not be looking for a short cut or easy answers by showing up at church, what is the appropriate role of the church in the life of a believer? To understand the nature and Biblical role of the church, you must begin by understanding the church is a spiritual reality functioning in a temporal environment. When Jesus was on earth he taught about the "Kingdom of God." He taught that the Kingdom of God is a spiritual realm, a spiritual reality. It's a world that is in this world – the temporal, physical, time and space world – but it is also in eternity, in God's forever realm, where the Father, Son and Holy Spirit reside now, in the past, and forever in the future. Thus the Kingdom is in this world but also not of this world. The Kingdom of God exists now but it is also yet to come.

The Church, like the Kingdom, is also a spiritual reality. The Church is the people of God; it is all those who love and obey Jesus, but it is not limited to this world. According to Hebrews 12, we are surrounded by a great cloud of witnesses, who have gone before us and who are cheering us on from their places in heaven. Somehow, according to God's economy, his church cuts across all racial and ethnic divides, it cuts across time, it cuts across politics, nations, and culture. The church is not limited to a particular geo-political organization that calls itself a church or hangs a sign out front which says, "First Church of Whatever."

The organizational or physical entities that call themselves "a church" in this world are many and varied. On one extreme there are those who have no connection with Jesus, they are simply religious, or they may even be a satanic cult trying to lure true believers away from the Lord. Jesus warned us to be wary of false teachers, who he described as wolves in sheep's clothing (Matthew 7:15). On the other end of the continuum are churches filled with believers, who faithfully nurture and encourage the disciples and carry out the mission of Jesus in this world. Yet, even these churches are a mixture of the divine and profane, of the spirit-filled and the fleshy, of gold and of dirt.

Jesus explains this paradox by telling a story about a farmer who went out and planted good seed in his fields. At night an enemy came and sowed weeds among his wheat. The servants discover this and want to go tear out all the weeds. The farmer told them to leave things alone. "While you are pulling the weeds, you may root up the wheat with them." He tells them to wait until the harvest – then the weeds will be burned and the wheat will be sent unto the barns. (Matthew 13:24-30) God knows exactly what is going on in the church. Even the best churches are a bit of a mixed bag. In the end at the final judgment, God will sort it all out. As believers our job is to be discerning. We have the Holy Spirit living in us. So "do not believe every spirit, but test the spirits to see whether they are from God, because many false prophets have gone out into the world." (1 John 4:1).

THE BIBLICAL DEFINITION OF CHURCH

According to Scripture, the Church is the people of God, under the headship of Jesus Christ, indwelt by the Holy Spirit, living out the Great Commandment and the Great Commission. Let's take a minute and unpack that definition.

The church, like the Trinity of Father, Son and Holy Spirit, is a relational entity. Just like God himself, the church is a people who can best be described as a missional community. God has designed us for relationship – it is built into our very nature as human beings. When we join God's family, he makes us a part of his incarnational mission. His goal is to redeem the earth and all the people in it. As a missional community, that becomes our goal as well.

As the people of God, the church is an amazingly diverse group of peoples, tribes, cultures, and individuals. Scripture uses the analogy of the physical body to explain how the church can work together effectively even though all of its individual parts are so different. Read the full description of God's design for the church in 1Cor:12:12-31 to learn more, but here is the conclusion. As the Body of Christ, Jesus is our head. He is the head of the church. It does not matter whether we are an eye or a toenail; we get our direction from Jesus. He calls the shots for us, both individually and corporately. Jesus' job is to lead, to set the agenda. Our job is to follow, to be lovingly obedient. So in the church, "Speaking the truth in love, we will in all things grow up into him who is the Head, that is, Christ. From him the whole body, joined and held together by every supporting ligament, grows and builds itself up in love, as each part does its work." (Ephesians 4:15-16)

The church is composed of people who have been redeemed by the blood sacrifice of Jesus. We are ultimately to be from every people group across the face of the earth. "You are all sons of God through faith in Christ Jesus, for all of you who were baptized into Christ have clothed yourselves with Christ. There is neither Jew nor Greek, slave nor free, male nor female, for you are all one in Christ Jesus." (Galatians 3:26-29) Obviously, we don't speak each other's languages, and even where we do, there can be great cultural differences between all the people of God. What binds us together and helps us communicate? The Holy Spirit. So Paul tells us, "The body is a unit, though it is made up of many parts; and though all its parts are many, they form one body. So it is with Christ. For we were all baptized by one Spirit into one body-whether Jews or Greeks, slave or free-and we were all given the one Spirit to drink." (1Cor 12:12-13)

So now we know that the church is the people of God, submitting to the leadership of Jesus and knit together by the indwelling Holy Spirit. There are two more characteristics, however, that are required to meet the Biblical definition of Church. "Living out the Great Commandment and the Great Commission" admittedly, sounds like a bit of Christian jargon, which I like to avoid. Both of these phrases cover two very important attributes that Jesus calls the church to demonstrate.

The Great Commandment is Jesus' instruction to all of his followers to love each other. "A new command I give you: Love one another. As I have loved you, so you must love one another. *By this all men will know that you are my disciples, if you love one another*." (John 13:34-35) There are many verses in both the Gospels and the rest of the New Testament which describe the importance of love between believers. The 285 direct commands I mentioned before are all just an elaboration on the kind of love that should characterize those who are Christ followers. This quality of love is one of the sure marks of a church which is part of God's Forever Family.

The Great Commission is a similar umbrella which covers a character trait of the church that spreads both broad and deep. This is the name given to the final address of Jesus to his followers before he ascended to heaven to sit at the right hand of the Father. "Then Jesus came to them and said, "All authority in heaven and on earth has been given to me. Therefore, go and make disciples of all nations, baptizing them in the name of the Father and of the Son and of the Holy Spirit, and teaching them to obey everything I have commanded you. And surely I am with you always, to the very end of the age." (Matthew 28:18-20) In this short passage, Jesus commissions his followers to pick up his incarnational mandate here on earth and to carry it out until this age ends. You cannot be the church if you are not living out Jesus' mission in the world.

The churches you might encounter are many and varied. There are large "mega churches" like Willow Creek Community Church near Chicago, The Potter's House in Dallas or Saddleback Valley Community Church in Orange County, CA each of which might have 20,000 to 30,000 people worshiping on a weekend. At the other end of the spectrum are the house churches of China. These typically have 10 to 20 people in them. Any larger than that and the authorities will discover them and put them out of business. So they stay small and multiply.

At the extreme, you could have a church of two people. Jesus promised, "If two of you on earth agree about anything you ask for, it will be done for you by my Father in heaven. For where two or three come together in my name, there am I with them." (Matthew 18:19-20) Regardless of their size or sophistication, a church must have these five characteristics to be the true church as Scripture defines it. The people of God, following the leadership of Jesus, indwelt by the Holy Spirit, living in love, and living out Jesus' mission.

PRACTICAL TIPS FOR FINDING A CHURCH

The health of the church universal, and its local manifestations vary from place to place. Worldwide the church is growing exponentially outside of the Western countries. In Asia, Africa and Latin America the church is healthy and vibrant. In Brazil the church is adding 20,000 new believers each week. In China the church is adding 20,000 to 30,000 new believers a day! On the other hand, the church in

Western Europe and North America has been stagnant or in decline for most of the last 100 years. I'm sorry to report that in the USA it is much easier to find a weak or dysfunctional church than it is to find a healthy congregation.

Currently, there are over 1,300 Protestant denominations in the USA. New believers (and other people with a modicum of sense) often ask, "Why are there so many divisions in the church, if Jesus calls us to be one in him?" Good question. In my opinion, most denominational divisions are caused by mankind's constant efforts to control God and other people. We want to keep God under control so he does not rock our world. So we create systems, theology, culture, and practices to keep our faith in a form we can manage. I don't think this is part of God's plan. In fact I'm pretty sure he wants to rock the boat until we put our faith in him rather than our own feeble efforts to direct our lives. No matter how many denominational boxes we create to control God, his Spirit will break out and do a new thing.

A few years ago, I did an interesting research project for a major Christian publisher. We segmented all 300,000 churches in the United States into four groups: Fundamentalist, Evangelical, Conservative Mainline, and Liberal Mainline. The outcome of the research showed the Liberal Mainline churches had significantly different views about Jesus and Scripture, but that the other three groups agreed on every point of basic doctrine and belief. So what made them different? Their culture! Issues like whether women could wear slacks to church, what translation of the Bible was preferred, where the pastor went to seminary, and where they sent their kids to college. There were so many differences dividing believers and almost none of them had to do with faith in Jesus.

My wife and I have moved 17 times during our 30 years of marriage, so we have had some little experience with looking for a church to call our own. While I confess I studied the field of Church Growth under the leading practitioners at Fuller Seminary, most of what I know about shopping for a church I learned in the "school of hard knocks." At one point when my kids were still preschool age, I took my family to 13 different churches 13 weeks in a row. What a grueling ordeal! I can't believe my family didn't desert me after the pain I inflicted running them through that gauntlet. Let me summarize a few key points I learned along the way that might help you find a church.

Leadership is critical. Does the Senior Pastor (and do other leaders you meet) demonstrate the love of Christ? Is the focus on Jesus and people he died to save, or is it on other issues? When the pastor speaks do you get a sense of God's grace and love or one of judgment? Is the focus on Jesus' mission or is it on social issues or political issues? Does he point people to Jesus with hope of healing, or does he warn you of enemies in our midst, people we need to attack? Corporate culture, in the church as well as any other organization, flows from the top down. If you don't get a good feeling about the Senior Pastor or other top leaders, look elsewhere.

Worship styles vary all over the map and that's fine. God loves variety and is able to work through any culture or style issues. Find a style you feel comfortable with. But check out the preaching and teaching. Is it Christ centered? Is it based on Scripture? Regardless of style, you want a church that lifts up Jesus and not other issues. If they talk a lot about politics, social issues, various popular causes or "isms" instead of Jesus – go elsewhere. You want a church that teaches people how to get connected and stay connected to Jesus.

How do the people treat you? That's how you will find out if the church is living the Great Commandment. Some of the most resilient congregations in America are actually made up of a dozen extended families that have been in that congregation for many decades or even generations. If that's the case, you are going to have a hard time breaking in and finding community. I remember one church we visited. There were about 250 in worship Sunday morning. We walked in and you could tell, they all knew we were the only strangers in the house. People kept staring at us like we had three heads. They kept staring and edging away. And no one, not even the pastor, came over and spoke to us during the entire morning.

You won't always know a lot of people right off, but ask yourself if these **are people you would like to get to know?** Do they look like people you would be comfortable hanging out with? The way people dress, their age and stage, the variety of types of people, the presence of internationals, the way they talk and laugh – these can all be signs that attract or repel you. It's ok to trust your feelings on this. That's one of the reasons why God gives you feelings. At another church we visited, we attended a Sunday school class with about 50 young married folks our age and stage. There was lots of mingling and talking. My initial impression was quite positive. Yet as we drove home I realized something was wrong. I liked all the wives but none of their husbands! Later I figured out what the problem was. Most of the men were chemical engineers and computer technicians. Their wives were their opposites (as they often are) – cheerful, gregarious, and verbal. Good for Martie; not so good for Bruce. We crossed it off the list.

Finally, you need to find out: **is this congregation pursuing Jesus' mission**, living out the Great Commission.? It has been rightly said that the church is the only club in the world that exists primarily for the benefit of those who don't belong. See if the church you are considering puts a high value on Jesus' mission. Are there active efforts to reach out and care for the poor, to visit the sick, to minister to those in need, to care for those in prison and to share the Good News with the spiritually hungry? And are you encouraged to join and participate in these efforts? Not everyone in a particular congregation will join in with caring for those outside, but the church, as a whole needs to put a high priority on mission and facilitate involvement for those who are serious about following Jesus.

Some churches have gradually become inwardly focused until they are actually consumer-driven organizations, a bit like the big box stores. People come for what they want, they take it, and leave. If you don't have what they want, they go elsewhere. If a church spends 80% or more of its efforts serving those already in the church, look elsewhere. The church the New Testament describes is a place where we are called to service, not just a place where we can be served.

Ultimately, you test the mission focus of a congregation exactly the way Jesus instructs us to in (Matthew 7:16-23). The question to ask, if I may paraphrase the old Wendy's commercial, is "Where's the fruit?" Some congregations give tremendous lip service to the mission of Christ, but have little if any fruit. Look at the budget. I came across a church that talked all the right talk about reaching the lost from the pulpit. However, in a church budget of $700,000 per year, they had only $400 set aside for outreach. They may have had great theological convictions, but there was no fruit. Look for people outside the church being helped and served, cared for, helped financially or in practical ways, and coming to faith in Jesus. Those are the visible signs of a mission driven church.

WHAT IF YOU CAN"T FIND A GOOD CHURCH?

Some of you will search and search without success for a local church that looks even vaguely like the church we've just described. Others of you may live in rural or remote communities where the churches you have access to are few and far between. None of the ones you can get to feel like a good fit for you. I had a reader write to me from a small farming town in the wheat fields of central Kansas. She said, "There are only five churches in my area. All of them are collections of various families who have 'run' that church as a private club for many years. There are different labels over the door – Lutheran, Presbyterian, Methodist, Baptist, and Mennonite – but they all suffer from being isolated, ingrown, and inbred without much love for Jesus."

Some of you may be in professions that require you to work on weekends, when most churches in America tend to have their weekly get-togethers. You might be a critical care nurse or you could sell time-share condos in a resort community or you could run a summer camp. Some would tell you to quit your job if you have to work on weekends, but Jesus told both tax collectors and soldiers not to change their jobs after coming to faith (Luke 3). The principle of incarnational ministry would tell us that, logically, God must want followers of Jesus in every line of work, including those that labor on Saturday and Sunday so that their co-workers can eventually hear the Good News.

Let me offer a few suggestions about how you might proceed to a solution. If you know of a good church but you have schedule conflicts, look for creative alternatives. Many churches offer evening meetings, both on Sunday and some weekdays as well. Willow Creek Community Church, for example, has their major time of teaching and fellowship for believers on Wednesday nights. Other churches might offer programs for various ages and stages at the church. There might be Bible studies, prayer meetings, or geographically dispersed small groups hosted by the church or individuals in it.

I met a man from Rhode Island whose functional church was actually a meeting of men that gathered every Friday morning a in downtown Providence tavern. A diverse group of business people, lawyers, politicians, and many others, the group initially was a small Bible study. More and more men wanted to come. As the group grew, the only meeting place they could find near enough to where most of the guys worked was a large bar. Well, why not? It was closed, and they were not serving alcohol. At this point about 80 men meet together every Friday morning to study, worship, share, and pray.

If you have trouble finding a church, you will begin to understand the value of being in community. While you are in process, community will sustain you. My friend Larry retired to a rural area a couple hours from his hometown. While he was looking for a new church, he started a prayer time with the one other guy he knew in the area. Every Monday night they got together, shared lives, had a devotional, and then prayed for each other. This fellowship has expanded, adding a couple of guys who work down in DC, an accountant; a heavy equipment operator, and a several retired men. Having a community of friends to encourage and support him enabled Larry to hang in there until he found a good church.

You may find yourself stumped. Don't worry, its ok. You have God on your side. He will help you find a fellowship of believers to plug into, although you may have to create it yourself. Pray about your situation and ask God what he wants you to do. Deb and Charlie Mathers had a hard time finding a church where they fit in rural Vermont. They developed a local small group and then began to network with other like-minded believers they knew in Northern New Hampshire and upstate New York. Eventually this network developed into a regional church of individuals and families. They meet once a month and rotate locations so people take turns driving. When they meet they invest the whole day so they have the opportunity to do a variety of things in their time together.

Why do you need a group larger than your small group, if that's where you experience community? I would not want to limit God's creativity and the variety of ways he can accomplish his purposes, but I see several advantages in a group that is larger. The first is the fact that God gives every believer at least one spiritual gift for the purpose of building up other believers. A small group of ten may meet your need for friends, but it won't have the broader cross section of gifts we need to grow to maturity in the faith. Another issue is opportunity for ministry and service. Small groups tend to be pretty homogeneous, with people from a similar age, stage and life situation. A larger group offers a greater variety of needs, people with diverse passions, and more opportunities to develop unique ministries. Finally, if you have kids, a larger group will have a more diverse mix of ages and personality among the other kids, providing better odds that your kids will find others they click with.

If you are having trouble finding a church, you might want to look for a ministry in your community appealing to you. Often believers, who share a similar burden about ministering to a particular need, have lots of other things in common. When I lived in the Lehigh Valley in Pennsylvania, we got involved with a group of adults who supported an evangelistic outreach in our area high schools. They became both our community and our functional church for a number of years. Depending on your interests, you might seek out people who are ministering in prisons, those who help unwed mothers, or handicapped adults. There may be a soup kitchen, a homeless shelter, or a coffee house for young people. Any of these might offer the chance to serve and the opportunity to meet like-minded believers who ultimately become your church.

Truthfully, it's not bad for you to be a little bit hungry for a good church. When I first became a believer, for the first year or so my only spiritual resource was prayer. But it was enough. I learned to talk to God, and I learned to listen to him as well. No one I had ever met who went to church talked about having a relationship with Jesus. I just did not know there was any connection. My second year of faith, a friend introduced me to the Bible. She said it was full of love letters from God to his followers. That was a big help in my growth. Later, I met a group of believers who were involved in ministry in my town. I joined in, learned to serve others, learned to pray, received Biblical teaching, developed community, and generally began to mature and deepen in my walk of faith. It was a total of five years before I went to a church and I don't think it had any negative impact on my growth. Jesus was always enough for me. He has never failed to provide what I needed to grow when I needed it. He is enough.

A WALK IN THE WILDERNESS

When Jesus began the public phase of his ministry here on earth, he spent 40 days in the wilderness being tested. (Matthew 4:1-11). In your spiritual life you will experience times of hardship and testing. Scripture suggests that may be part of God's strategy to draw us to him, to teach us to depend on him alone, and to learn the road to maturity – trust and obedience. This may be your experience in searching for a church home. Scripture urges us to seek such a home. "And let us consider how we may spur one another on toward love and good deeds. Let us not give up meeting together, as some are in the habit of doing, but let us encourage one another…" (Hebrews 10:24-25)

At the same time, I want to urge you not to settle for less than what God wants for you in a church. Do not continue to go to a church that makes you feel pressured, threatened, or coerced into accepting someone else's point of view. If you feel you have to compromise your faith in order to be accepted by people in a church, you need to get out of there. This is how cults start. If a congregation's love seems conditional, if it's only offered to those who buy into a prescribed political point of view, it's not a place where you will be able to grow in Christ. Jesus offers us grace, room to grow, the freedom to be ourselves, and the "peace that passes understanding." If you are not finding that in a church, it's better to do without.

Jesus also warns us to avoid churches that are just going through the motions. Some churches simply come together to worship, they have no mission, and it's all about serving those already inside the club. This is not a neutral environment, although that's how it might feel at times. Listen to what Jesus says to the church at Laodicea, "I know your deeds, that you are neither cold nor hot. I wish you were either one or the other! So, because you are lukewarm-neither hot nor cold - I am about to spit you out of my mouth." (Rev 3:15-16) If you find yourself in such a church, you need to get out. It will cause you pain and struggle. People may not understand. But you will be better off in the wilderness with Jesus until he gives you another solution, than safely in a church Jesus ultimately disowns. Remember, Jesus will provide everything you need. He is enough.

FAITH IS A JOURNEY

"Life is difficult." Author and psychologist Scott Peck begins his book, _The Road Less Traveled_, with this line. It is a simple but profound truth. If you have not yet gone through trouble or tragedy, it is waiting for you down the road. Here is what you need to know. You can practice each of the six disciplines, and I hope you will. You can master these disciplines and have a very tight walk with Jesus. After all that, you can still go through very hard times.

If you study the teachings of Jesus, you will find two promises occur repeatedly. He tells his followers they will have difficulties, persecution, and a variety of troubles. He also promises to see us through all of these hard experiences. Here are both of his promises in one verse. "I have told you these things, so that in me you may have peace. In this world you will have trouble. But take heart! I have overcome the world." (John 16:33)

As a follower of Jesus Christ, we reap many benefits from walking with him in this life. We have forgiveness of sin, relationship with God, eternal salvation to come, joy, peace, our friends in the Forever Family, and countless other blessings. That does not mean our life will be all peace and prosperity from now on. No matter how strong our walk with God, things may happen which completely pull the rug out from underneath our faith.

There are times in your walk with Jesus where life just eats away at you. No great crisis or tragedy, but a series of clouds come over your horizon until you look up and ask, "How did it get so dark all of a sudden?" This past summer was a time like that for me. I helped both of my daughters' graduate and move to new cities where they have each started very interesting professional careers. But as a Daddy, I can't help but mourn the loss of my little girls. My wife's frail 92-year-old father has had a number of fainting and falling incidences, which required sudden trips to Pittsburgh to help with doctors and hospitals.

My own father's health declined to the point where we had to move him into a retirement community. My brother and I made many trips driving back and forth to Philadelphia to facilitate the move and deal with 80 years of accumulated stuff. Finally, in August, my mother died suddenly. She knew the Lord, was not in good health, so it was really a blessing, but still it came as a shock. By mid August, I found myself deeply depressed and discouraged, hardly able to comprehend why the sun bothered to come up in the morning. When I tried to pray, it was if the ceiling was lined with lead – nothing going up and nothing coming back.

There will be times in your walk of faith when you lose direction and are not sure what to do. Perhaps you have choices you need to make or you are seeking God's direction for some area of your life, but everything is dark. You just don't know what to do. George MacDonald, the famous Scottish writer and preacher, offers this advice. "For a man is not bound to walk in the dark, but only to wait until the light comes. Neither must he act, merely for the sake of doing something and thus run the risk of doing something wrong. He that believes shall not make haste."

Even those who vigorously pursue the Lord, who have high aspirations for service in God's Kingdom, sometimes find themselves stymied. We feel a sense of call to a particular mission or need, we have a passion to minister to those people with that need, we have the gifts and skills to succeed in that work – and yet, at times, it seems like God himself is keeping the door closed. For years I have read Psalm 37:4, "Delight yourself in the Lord, and He will give you the desires of your heart." Then I wonder why God has not been a little more prompt in giving me the desires of my heart, especially in areas of ministry. Of course, if you read the rest of that Psalm there are multiple mentions of "waiting for the Lord" which I sometimes overlook. God's timing is perfect and we need to learn to wait for it. The waiting process helps us mature.

Then there are times of genuine hardship. Look at the Apostle Paul. He was a giant of the faith, but listen to a few of the hardships he walked through. "Five times I received from the Jews the 40 lashes minus one. Three times I was beaten with rods, once I was stoned, three times I was shipwrecked, I spent a night and a day in the open sea, I have been constantly on the move. I have been in danger from rivers, in danger from bandits, in danger from my own countrymen, in danger from Gentiles; in danger in the city, in danger in the country, in danger at sea; and in danger from false brothers. I have labored and toiled and have often gone without sleep; I have known hunger and thirst and have often gone without food; I have been cold and naked. Besides everything else, I face daily the pressure of my concern for all the churches." (2 Cor 11:24-28) Hardly sounds like a walk in the park, does it?

Many other men and women of faith testify that they too have experienced tragedy, trials and testing, periods of time that might be called "the dark night of the soul." Mother Teresa, perhaps the most famous missionary to the poor in our age and a giant of the faith, was afflicted with feelings of abandonment by God through much of her adult life. Quotes from her journals include these: "I am told that God lives in me – and yet the reality of darkness and coldness and emptiness is so great that nothing touches my soul." "I want God with all the power of my soul – and yet between us there is a terrible separation." "Heaven is from every side closed."

Dr. Larry Crabb is a licensed psychotherapist, a noted author of 15 books on Biblical principles for marriage, relationships, inner healing and counseling, as well as a Professor at Colorado Christian University. He shares about a recent struggle he had with depression and despair. "God is stripping me of much I've depended on for my sense of well being…my soul is ripped apart, filled with desolation and despair, made raw, lacerated. It longs for a healing that no one can arrange. It is a season of absolute vulnerability before God. If he does nothing, there will be no resurrection, only ongoing death…" [20]

In your own life, you may go through the deep water. The trials and tragedies of life have a profound role to play in our spiritual development. God does not send these things our way (James 1), but in his mercy he uses the circumstances of life to help us mature in him. When life tosses the tough stuff at us, we either become better people or we become bitter people. To some extent, your response may depend on how well you have applied the six disciplines to develop your walk with God. The better you know him, the better connected you are to others who know him, the better equipped you will be to weather the storms of life.

Remember, nothing can separate us from the love of God. "For I am convinced that neither death nor life, neither angels nor demons, neither the present nor the future, nor any powers, neither height nor depth, nor anything else in all creation, will be able to separate us from the love of God that is in Christ Jesus our Lord." (Romans 8:38-39) God will hold your hand through every trial and temptation and will not let you fall. A verse that has sustained me through many dark and hard times is 1 Cor 10:13 – "No trial has overcome you except what is common to man. And God is faithful; he will not let you be tested beyond what you can bear. But when you are tested, he will also provide a way out so that you can stand up under it." This has been the knot at the end of my rope that enabled me to hang on to God on many occasions.

IS JESUS ENOUGH?

At the beginning of this book I said that faith is a journey, not a destination. I imagine your own walk of faith will provide ample evidence that this is true. God is real, and he makes himself known to us in the most intimate details of our lives. As your experience with the Lord increases, you will be amazed at the quiet yet grace filled ways he injects himself in your life. There are many promises in God's Word, and all of them will come true. These promises are so cool that one

publisher has compiled them into a neat little paperback book. I keep one by my
bedside and refer to it often just to remind me of the good things God has done, is
doing and will do in my life. (See Appendix)

At the same time life is full of profound mysteries. There is much about
God, an infinite, unlimited, supernatural, spiritual being that we finite and limited
human beings will never understand. There is also a great deal about living in a
sinful fallen world that we don't understand. There is much tragedy that occurs
which is no one's fault, but is a consequence of our mortal enemy Satan, who
prowls the world causing mayhem and destruction. Even in our own lives, we see
victories and failures, growth and collapse, spiritual maturity and moral failure.
We are works in progress – clearly in God's hands and headed his way, but prone
to all sorts of setbacks.

Learn the six disciplines of following Jesus. I urge you to seek him out
every day and apply his teaching to your life. I know that you will experience
profound blessing and encouragement as you walk with him and grow in faith.
These disciplines will make you strong and resilient so you can overcome the
storms of life. The Lord's goal for each of us is to help us mature so we reflect his
love to those around us, become a beacon of hope in a dark world, and eventually
become more and more like Jesus. His desire is that when we finally arrive in his
presence by the Father's side, he can say, "Well done thou good and faithful
servant."

Dr. Marvin Wilson, a noted Old Testament scholar and Bible professor at
Gordon College, once gave me this profound little word of advice. "When your
theology and your experience of God conflict; throw out your theology." Our
theology, our thinking about God and our understanding of Him, often comes up
short. We simply have trouble understanding much of what there is to know about
God. But God himself is love. He loves you, and he will not let you down. Even
when you do not understand what is going on in your life or what he is trying to do
with you, trust him. He is faithful. He will not let you down.

Jed Wickham is a dedicated believer. He applied himself to a career in
higher education, finishing with a PhD from the University of Michigan. He
worked his way up through the ranks to become a tenured professor at Michigan
State University. His field of expertise was the application of innovation. This led

to his appointment as the president of a medium-sized auto supplier. Both his reputation and the financial rewards continued to increase.

Active in his church, he served in ministry both in the church and community. In mid-career he was asked serve in the administration of a Christian college in his home state. Following several important promotions, he was made president of the college. Three years later, without any warning, the Board of the college fired him. At age 55, for the first time in his life, Jed Wickham was out on the street without a job.

The next three years were a nightmare. He knocked on hundreds of doors and sent out many resumes. He tried everything he could think of but could not land a job. Not in teaching or administration or in manufacturing. All his accomplishments and successes seemed worthless. No one would give him a chance. Finally, one afternoon as he was walking and crying out in his pain to the Lord, Wickham heard Jesus say, "Am I enough? Am I enough for you, Jed?"

When the tough times of life hit, that is the question each of us needs to answer. Is Jesus enough? When all else I depend on is stripped away, will I cling to Jesus as my hope and promise for a better future? Make Jesus the bedrock of your faith. Put your complete trust in Him. He will get you through today and will see you all the way home.

Discussion Questions – Chapter 12

1) Was there a time in your life when you thought faith was a yes or no proposition? You are either in or out?

2) How do you react to this quote: "Faith is a journey, not a destination?" Explain your answer.

3) Was there a part of the reading in this chapter about finding a church that was particularly helpful for you, that made a connection in your mind, or that you disagree with? Share about that.

4) Have you ever had a bad experience in a church? Would you be willing to share a little of what you learned, from that experience, with the group?

5) Do you know of other Christians and ministries in your community that are not part of your congregation? Would you be willing to befriend and support any of these? Explain your answer.

6) Have you ever struggled with depression? What helps you get better when you are down or discouraged?

7) Was there a part of the reading in this chapter that was particularly helpful for you, that made a connection in your mind, or that you disagree with? Share about that.

8) How might you use what you learned in this chapter to change your life in the coming week or months?

A P P E N D I X

Resources for Growth

Books to Nurture Your Faith:

- *Mere Christianity* by C.S. Lewis
- *Exploring God without Getting Religious* by Bruce R. Dreisbach
- *The Case for Christ* by Lee Stroble
- *Christianity for Skeptics* by Steve Kumar
- *Christianity is Jewish* by Eve Shaefer
- *Passion & Purity* and *Shadow of the Almighty* by Elizabeth Elliott
- *Traveling Light*, by Max Lucado
- *Wild at Heart* (a book for men) by John Eldridge
- *Questions of Life* by Nicki Gumbal

Books on Marriage:

- *His Needs, Her Needs* by Williard F. Harley, Jr.
- *Making Love Last Forever* by Gary Smalley
- *Love and Respect* by Emerson Eggeriches

Books on Personal Disciplines:

- *Discovering the Spiritual Life* by Jeff Caliquire/Joe McGarry
- *Descending Like a Dove (the Holy Spirit)* by Clive Calver
- *Disappointment with God* by Philip Yancey
- *Hearing God* by Dallas Willard
- *Too Busy Not To Pray* by Bill Hybels
- *The Practice of the Presence of God* by Brother Lawrence
- *Decision Making and the Will of God* by Garry Friesen
- *Honesty, Morality and Conscience* by Jerry White
- *Wild Goose Chase* by Mark Batterson
- *What Jesus Meant* by Garry Wills

Books on Sharing Faith:

- *More Ready Than You Realize* by Brian D. McLaren
- *The Insider* by Jim Petersen & Mike Shamy
- *Out of the Belly of the Whale* by Bruce Roberts Dreisbach
- *Just Walk Across the Room* by Bill Hybels
- *Roaring Lambs* by Bob Briner
- *Going Public With Your Faith* by William Carr Peel & Walt Larimore
- *Seeker Small Groups* by Garry Poole

Other Resources:

- Soul Care (www.soulcare.com)
- Willow Creek Resource Center (www.seeds.willowcreek.org/wc/)
- Walk Through the Bible (www.walkthru.org).
- Willow Creek Association (www.willowcreek.com)
- Youth With A Mission (YWAM) (www.ywam.org)

Scripture Passages by Topic or Need:

These short volumes list helpful verses or passages from God's Word by the specific need, such as fear, comfort, guidance, temptation, forgiveness, etc.

- *The Jesus Person Promise Book,* Edited by David Wilkerson, 1972, Regal Books, Gospel Light, Ventura, CA.

- *The Living Bible Promise Book,* 1988, Barbour Books, Westwood, NJ.
- *Quick Scripture Reference for Counseling,* John G. Kruis, 1988, Baker Books House, MI.

Sharing the Gospel - The Bridge Illustration

Gospel Presentation: "The Bridge," a tool developed by the Navigators Ministry

God wants to have a relationship with us.

However, we have rebelled against Him and broken off that relationship

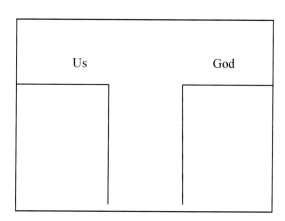

Most of us are aware
of this and try *to do*
things to get back with
God, but it doesn't work.

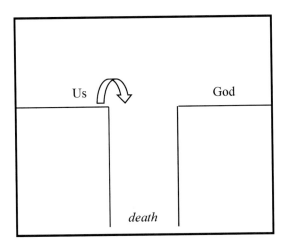

But God did for us
what we could not do,
and that is build a bridge
back to Himself.

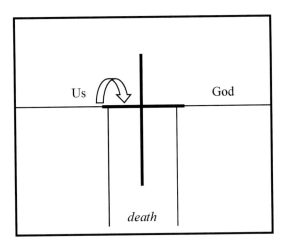

He did that by paying
our death penalty
when He died on the
cross.

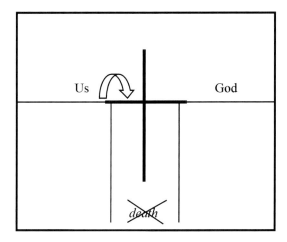

One last thing. It is not
enough just to know this.
We must act on it by
admitting that we have
rebelled and by asking
God for His forgiveness
and leadership.

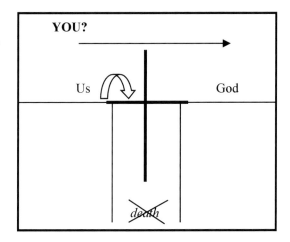

Conclude by asking your
friend where they think
they are on the diagram.

Growing with God